Praise fo

Th...

Gómez Dávila ranks with Guénon and Evola in his insight into the "reign of quantity" and his "revolt against the modern world." Aphorisms fired off half a century ago hit the bullseye in our era, as Ramon Elani's indispensable glosses demonstrate.

—Joscelyn Godwin, author of *Harmonies of Heaven and Earth*, *Atlantis and the Cycles of Time*, etc.

Aphorisms are a genre of which Nicolás Gómez Dávila was a master, and in this thematic selection and commentary, Ramon Elani ably explicates Dávila's mordant critiques of an age of decline.

—Arthur Versluis, Hieros Institute, author of *American Gnosis*, *The Mystical State*, and other books

Dávila presents a Traditionalist European view spoken through the lens of postcolonial South America. He is a voice for many in our times that tells us not to seek solutions to the world's myriad of problems, but to hold fast to our core principles. An aristocrat in the true sense of the word, Dávila promotes greatness, honor, defense of culture, and a recognition of one's place in the cosmos. He philosophically dismantles the false promises of egalitarianism, technology, democracy, and the rampant political doctrines aimed at worldwide "salvation," consumer capitalism and communism. Like a modern Montaigne, he provides a guide, a map, on how to live and to be amidst the noise of the world, performing one's duties with dignity and surrendering oneself into the hands of the Divine.

This book came to me at the right time, and I believe that if you are reading this, then it has come to you at the right time as well. Read it well, read it deeply, do not imitate it slavishly, but enjoy its aphorisms and insights as one does a gourmet meal in each of its stages.

—Mark Stavish, Director of Studies, Institute for Hermetic Studies, and author of *Egregores* and *The Path of Freemasonry*

Gómez Dávila's aphorisms are a rare instance of an authentic excoriation of the structural failings of the modernist project that were apparent to a few thinking people in his time and are even more relevant today.

—Nigel Pennick, author of *The Eldritch World*, *The Book of Primal Signs*, etc.

Dávila wasn't only a philosopher, a theologian, and a prophet: he was also a poet. *The Authentic Reactionary* is an intellectual and aesthetic feast. Read it slowly; savor every "gloss." Then, when you're done, read it again.

—Michael Warren Davis, author of *The Reactionary Mind*

For Nicolás Gómez Dávila, "it is the progress of progress that forces us to be reactionary." This is why he defined himself as an anti-modern and an "authentic reactionary"—one who made philosophy a way of life. Little known during his lifetime, the Colombian author today has a large number of readers in France, Germany, Italy, and Spain. Until now he has been ignored in the English-speaking world—which is not surprising, as the latter is won over to the mythology of "progress." Everyone, however, can benefit from these writings: one must read Gómez Dávila to understand what an intelligent reactionary is.

—Alain de Benoist, author of *On Being a Pagan*, *The Empire of Myth*, etc.

Ramon Elani has performed an heroic feat in translating these scholia of the Colombian thinker Nicolás Gómez Dávila and making them available to English-speaking readers. Gómez Dávila, whose philosophy is almost an anti-philosophy, offers an alternative to the dull pendular oscillations of the academy and cuts to the bone of academic and philosophical discourse, exposing its pretensions and performances and laying bare its utter banality. In that, alone, this is a welcome and refreshing volume. In addition, Elani's perspicacious commentary is a fitting complement to the work of this great mind.

—Michael Martin, Director, The Center for Sophiological Studies, and author of *The Submerged Reality* and *Transfiguration*

Writers and Philosophers on Nicolás Gómez Dávila

If I were not a communist, I would think like him in every way.

—Gabriel García Márquez

I salute you from across the trenches!

—Heiner Müller, in a dedication written to Gómez Dávila

A renowned unknown.

—José Miguel Oviedo, Peruvian author of the *Historia de la literatura hispanoamericana*

I know of no earlier example of a more lucid and beautiful style in Spanish.

—Álvaro Mutis, Columbian author of *The Adventures and Misadventures of Maqroll*

A Columbian Nietzsche . . . Gómez Dávila is undoubtedly one of the most original recluses of the twentieth century, who has shown us the role of the philosopher-author in the modern world. In an incomparable style, he simultaneously cultivates the legacy of ancient Greece and the spirit of Chartres.

—Franco Volpi, Italian philosopher and historian of philosophy

His thinking reveals itself as a tightly packed emergency kit for an indefinite stay in icy regions.

—Martin Mosebach, German author of *The Heresy of Formlessness* and *The 21: A Journey into the Land of the Coptic Martyrs*

Nicolás Gómez Dávila has written the best aphorisms of the twentieth century.

—Robert Spaemann, German Catholic philosopher and bioethicist, author of *Happiness and Benevolence*

A reliable old European.

—Gerd-Klaus Kaltenbrunner, Austrian philosopher and author of *Vom Geist Europas*

The reactionary is the last fantasist in a complete fantasy world.

—Botho Strauß, German playwright and novelist

In his *Escolios*, Gómez Dávila has bequeathed to us a whole series of small masterpieces of uncompromising ingenuity, and that is enough for him to be counted among the great aphorists.

—Werner Helmich, professor emeritus of Romance Languages and Literature, University of Graz

Critics on Nicolás Gómez Dávila

In the 1990s Dávila's aphorisms circulated among a few conservative thinkers; today their collective attack on the disenchanted world is attracting more and more readers. . . . Dávila's apodictic style provides no constructive criticism with respect to the present; he simply rejects it. His aphorisms are marked by an aesthetic and religious revulsion at the transformation of man into a consumer.

—Doja Hacker, *Der Spiegel*

Amid the flood of shallow writings, Dávila's philosophy stands like a reef.

—Manfred Lange, *Die Tagespost*

For his admirers, the existence of this philosopher must seem like a miracle in the midst of the catastrophe.

—Malte Oppermann, *Die Tagespost*

Whoever starts quoting him won't be able to stop.

—Michael Klonovsky, *Focus*

An enemy of any illusionary expectations of politics embellished by cheap optimism. . . . Gómez Dávila thus considers stupidity and ignorance to be crimes. Philosophy, on the other hand, has as its true task to create an awareness of the unsolvability of problems—to make the problems we face recognizable as such.

—Julius Möllenbach, *Junge Freiheit*

While Gómez Dávila criticizes democracy without hesitation, he does so in the name of individual liberty. . . . When all is said and done, [his] writings are most likely meant as an attempt to wake up the reader from the banalities of homogeneity.

—Virgil Nemoianu, *Modern Language Notes*

Gómez Dávila did not respond to the thought of others; rather, he forged his own path, as personal as could be. . . . The quantity and diversity of the thought collected in the scholia is inexhaustible.

—Nelson Rivera, *Latin American Literature Today*

It is fitting that one of the most profound thinkers of the twentieth century should also have been one of its most obscure. . . . Today, the prescience of Dávila's words is readily apparent. To protect against the chimerical threats posed by everything from global pandemics to destabilizing cyberattacks, modern man is proving all too willing to sacrifice what remains of his sovereignty on the altar of an ever-expanding administrative state premised on technocratic management and control.

—Matthew Pheneger, *The Imaginative Conservative*

Gómez Dávila's aphorisms open new intellectual and spiritual possibilities for the reactionary or conservative thinker, as his writings, like (good) poetry, reveal their truth gradually.

—Nayeli Riano, *The Imaginative Conservative*

His minute reflections on aesthetics, politics, and theology are rewarding out of all proportion to their length.

—Matthew Walther, *First Things*

Dávila despised rationalists, stripped progress bare, ridiculed democracy, and blasted the new secular religion imposed by an omnipresent state. But he was not just a stick of dynamite caught alight. He also found kindness, peace, and humor. He loved literature and language. He loved God. All his work seemed to be a melancholy homage to the vanished world of his childhood, an ode to tradition.

—Itxu Díaz, *The American Conservative*

The Authentic Reactionary

The Authentic Reactionary: Selected Scholia of Nicolás Gómez Dávila
Translated with commentary by Ramon Elani
ISBN: 979-8-9862234-1-4

Edited by Michael Moynihan and Joshua Buckley.
Interior layout by Joshua Buckley.
Cover design by Arcana Europa & Autumnos Studio.
Cover painting: *A Walk at Dusk* by Caspar David Friedrich, ca. 1830–1835. Courtesy of the Getty Museum.
Back cover and interior photographs of Nicolás Gómez Dávila courtesy of Karolinger Verlag.
Additional translation credits—Epigraph page: Seneca quote from his letter to Lucilius, §58.3, translated by Richard M. Gummere; Persius quote translated by Ramon Elani; Ludwig Klages quote translated by Michael Moynihan. Page xxxii: Eichendorff quote translated by Michael Moynihan.

The publisher thanks Dr. Till Kinzel, Sean Tejaratchi, and Dr. Peter Weiß.

Arcana Europa Media
P. O. Box 6115
North Augusta, SC 29861

www.arcanaeuropamedia.com

The Authentic Reactionary

Selected Scholia of Nicolás Gómez Dávila

Translated with commentary by Ramon Elani

ARCANA EUROPA

Nicolás Gómez Dávila

Contents

Why will no man confess his faults? Because he is still in their grasp; only he who is awake can recount his dream, and similarly a confession of sin is a proof of sound mind.
—Seneca

And no one dares to descend into himself, no one!
—Persius, *Satires*, IV, 23

It is the nature of all greatness not to be exact.
—Edmund Burke, "First Speech on the Conciliation with America"

That Jones shall worship the god within him turns out ultimately to mean that Jones shall worship Jones. Let Jones worship the sun or moon, anything rather than the Inner Light; let Jones worship cats or crocodiles, if he can find any in his street, but not the god within.
—G. K. Chesterton, *Orthodoxy*

"Progress" sweeps over the Earth like a ravenous blaze, and the places it has scorched will never thrive again, as long as men live. The extinguished species of animals and plants will not renew themselves; mankind's quiet warm-heartedness has been consumed; the wellspring within, which once nourished the blossoming songs and sacred festivals, is sealed up; and all that remains is the cold and dreary working day, bedecked with the fake tinsel of noisy "entertainment." Make no mistake: we are living in the age of the *downfall of the soul.*
—Ludwig Klages, *Mensch und Erde*

Foreword
A Hunter of Sacred Shadows Emerges into the Light

Till Kinzel

What seems to be improbable, may still occur. And it was surely quite improbable that a reclusive writer living in the shadows of the Andes in postcolonial Colombia would become a household name among avid readers in faraway countries like Austria, Germany, Italy, France, the Netherlands, Poland, Hungary, and even Russia. That something like this should happen is especially surprising—and must have been all the more so to the writer himself, Nicolás Gómez Dávila—in light of the contents of his work.

As someone vehemently opposed to almost all that is associated with the triumphs of modernity, Gómez Dávila was an odd choice to read in European countries, which in so many ways wanted to be absolutely modern. Here was a writer who stared resolutely into the face of the modern world and keenly discerned a set of features that were anything but attractive, let alone beautiful.

Must one swallow the tenets of progressivism without demurrals, or is it feasible—perhaps even necessary—for us to give voice to certain misgivings and dissent? To be sure, no society is perfect, and the wish to make them so can only be described as utopian hubris. But modern societies, and particularly their leaders, often find it hard to resist the temptation to claim that *this*, *here and now*, is the best society we have ever had. How lucky we are! But are we also happy? Not so much, avers Gómez Dávila. And since a certain discontent with the way things were headed did begin to arise toward the end of the twentieth century, at least in Europe, it was fitting that an attempt was made to probe deeper into the perplexities of life in what has often been described as "late modernity."

A small circle of independent-minded thinkers and writers discovered the pithy style and the sarcastic humor of Gómez Dávila with increasing enjoyment, using quotes from his writings to signal to their contemporaries that no matter how triumphantly modernity presented itself, it could not possibly be—nor could it ever provide—the final yardstick according to which values and well-being are measured. This pertains most particularly to everything connected to the human soul and its claims to beauty and truth.

In this sense, then, the improbability of the success of Gómez Dávila in Europe—and now perhaps even in North America and the rest of the English-speaking world—points tentatively to the possibility that future generations will not completely lose sight of the traditions of the West and the riches they contain. But this will only come about if the future generations also understand the gravity of our situation, in which the most fundamental concepts of these traditions are under relentless attack.

Nicolás Gómez Dávila is a most reliable guide in such matters, and accordingly should be studied not only with great care but with equally great passion. For even if we should ultimately fail to preserve Western civilization, there will be no excuse for not having tried to breathe new life into old truths about God, Man, and the World.

Till Kinzel, PhD, is the author of *Nicolás Gómez Dávila: Parteigänger verlorener Sachen* (NGD: Loyal Supporter of Lost Causes), which first appeared in 2003 and is now in its fifth revised and expanded edition (Rückersdorf: Lepanto, 2023). His other monographs include *Platonische Kulturkritik in Amerika: Studien zu Allan Blooms "The Closing of the American Mind"* (2002), *Michael Oakeshott: Philosoph der Politik* (2007), and *Johann Georg Hamann: Zu Werk und Leben* (2019), and he has published numerous essays on world literature. Recently he edited and translated Sir Walter Scott's *E. T. A. Hoffmann und das Übernatürliche*, with commentary (2022).

Nicolás Gómez Dávila:
A Concentric Soul in Search of Divine Wisdom

Ramon Elani

When I first encountered the words of Nicolás Gómez Dávila—a random if life-changing encounter—I had the overwhelming sensation of hearing an intimately familiar voice speaking to me from the furthest reaches of my soul. And this voice spoke not from the past, but from the domain of the timeless and eternal. With remarkable brevity and clarity, Gómez Dávila articulated isolated and fragmented thoughts that had long since been floating through my mind—sneaking suspicions, secret and frightening implications, agonizing yearnings. There is nothing "confessional" about Gómez Dávila's work except for this feeling of intimacy, the extraordinary experience of one soul speaking directly to another. These haunting words rise up out of nothing with all the potency of a phantom silently indicating the truth, like Banquo's ghost.

Our world is unraveling. It seems that every day brings with it some new threat, a new symptom of a general and fundamental problem. The members of contemporary society barely have time to come to terms with a crisis before a new one arises. Catastrophe piles upon catastrophe. The totalizing global domination of capitalism; the coming of a climate apocalypse that none of us are prepared for; the resurgent threat of nuclear war; increasing social breakdown marked by shocking acts of random and senseless violence, depression, and alienation; a new rise of nationalism and populism led by cruel and calculating demagogues, which hearkens back to the totalitarian horrors of the twentieth century; and the ceaseless development of new technologies that threaten the very essence of our humanity. In the face of such challenges, we are told everywhere and by every ideological faction that we are obligated *to act*. Everyone has such a clear sense of who or what is to blame, and what must be done to right the ship. Faced with such danger and uncertainty, humanity only becomes more certain, more close-minded, more urgent, and more hysterical. Humanity is tearing itself apart. In this atmosphere of chaos, the voice of Nicolás Gómez Dávila speaks to us calmly and dispassionately. Things are not what they seem. The cause lies elsewhere. We don't need solutions to these problems—we have plenty of those.

Solutions are attractive because they tell us what to do, which allows us to stop thinking. What we need today is what the greatest minds of history have tried to accomplish, and it is a simple thing. We need to understand ourselves. Without understanding or knowledge of the self, all our efforts will come to nothing. We need to heal ourselves. Modern humanity suffers chiefly from a malady of the soul. And above all else, what this wisdom and healing will demonstrate to us is that as horrifying as the threats we now face assuredly are, they are not new. The world has died and been reborn countless times. History does not begin with us, and it will not end with us. The wisdom of the classics, almost completely forgotten in this new dark age, is so shocking and so revelatory because it is all so familiar. We are not dealing with any problems that Cicero or Marcus Aurelius did not grapple with as well. There is nothing new under the sun. This is our blessing and our curse. And it is, above all, the main idea that Gómez Dávila sought to convey.

What we moderns need to understand, which the traditional wisdom of all historical epochs has tried to demonstrate, is that humanity cannot cure itself by its own means. What we really see when we try to understand what we are, is that we are not in control. To understand the human self is to acknowledge that we are not masters but slaves. The old pagans knew this, as do a handful of truly religious souls today. We don't need solutions, we don't need action—we need clarity to understand the true nature of the problem. Only a proper diagnosis can lead us to the correct treatment, and this is what Gómez Dávila attempted to provide.

Perhaps there is another world where Gómez Dávila is remembered as one of the most powerful reactionary, anti-modern, anti-industrial, anti-technology, anti-capitalist thinkers of the twentieth century. A world where his words have inspired millions and offered the solace of wisdom to this dark age. But that world is not this world, and my efforts in this volume are not motivated by changing that fact. There is good reason for this world to have forgotten Gómez Dávila, and he himself had no desire not to be forgotten. The reason is that every iota of Gómez Dávila's being and every word he ever wrote was in violent, rebellious, opposition to this world. Moreover, the nature of that hostility, which is increasingly rare and perhaps defines his work more than anything else, utterly precludes any attempt to act or change the world. As he frequently observed and as we have already remarked, the modern world is drowning in solutions. He staunchly refused to offer any. As we shall see in what follows, Gómez Dávila offered only an articulation of timeless truths and advocated nothing other than withdrawal.

Gómez Dávila's work is almost totally unknown in the English-speaking world, aside from a handful of online articles, amateur websites, and Twitter accounts. The same is true in his native Colombia and in other Spanish-speaking nations. The only exception is in Europe, particularly in Germany, where there has been some attempt at scholarly analysis and where all his major works have been translated. The one previous English translation of Gómez Dávila is a bilingual edition published in 2013 by the Columbian publisher Villegas Editores;[1] the book, which is difficult to find, unfortunately also fails to capture the spirit of Gómez Dávila's remarkable style and tone.

The facts of Nicolás Gómez Dávila's life (1913–1994) are quickly recounted and do little to illuminate his genius. This is, of course, highly fitting for one who sees himself as a transmitter of perennial truth. Gómez Dávila's historical circumstances explain little about his perspective precisely because, like Montaigne, he largely sought to separate his thoughts from the transient flux of geography, class, and history. Instead, he aimed to gesture toward that which is eternal.

1. *Scholia to an Implicit Text*, trans. Robert Pinzón (Bogotá: Villegas, 2013).

Gómez Dávila's life was not interesting; he did not seek success, nor did he achieve it. In his biography we perceive none of the restlessness, agitation, and neurosis so common to the thinkers of our time. Gómez Dávila stuck rigidly to a set of fixed habits and routines that remained intact for more than half a century.

Born in Bogotá in 1913, Gómez Dávila spent almost his entire life in Colombia. His father, a wealthy landowner who had added to his fortunes through commercial success in imported goods, could trace his ancestry back to the origins of the republic. While a genuine aristocracy never existed in the colonies, Gómez Dávila's Spanish heritage and the role of his ancestors in the Colombian struggle for independence placed him in an elite class both economically and socially.

When Gómez Dávila was a young boy, his family moved to Paris in order to provide him with an education beyond what he could expect to receive in Colombia. In Paris, he was instructed by Benedictine monks, but it appears that the most significant moment in his education occurred in 1929, at the age of sixteen, when he fell ill with pneumonia and was bedridden for two years. During this prolonged period of outward inactivity, Gómez Dávila focused all his energies on reading and the study of classical languages, foreshadowing a lifelong habit. In his unpublished master's thesis on Gómez Dávila, Mauricio Galindo Hurtado speculates on the impact which the political and cultural climate in Paris may have had on the young convalescent during this period.[2] Two significant cultural developments in French society are relevant here: Action Française and the Catholic Revival movement. Before discussing these movements, however, it is important to stipulate that the young Gómez Dávila, confined to his bed, almost certainly was not involved in any political or cultural groups, and it is unlikely that he met any of their leaders. We do know, however, that Gómez Dávila read much of the literature of both Action Française and the Catholic Revival, and their impact on his later thought is plain enough to see.

The primary motivation of the Action Française was an ultranationalistic monarchism, which sought the reestablishment

2. Galindo Hurtado, "A Reactionary in the Andes." My thanks to Dr. Till Kinzel for assistance in obtaining a copy of this thesis.

of order in an increasingly fragmented society. While Gómez Dávila would ultimately side more with the ideal of the aristocratic class, rather than the monarch, the overwhelming condemnation of democracy and the lament over the lost sense of integral order found in Action Française was certainly an enormous inspiration to the young Gómez Dávila. It is important to mention that Gómez Dávila's first book, *Notas* (Notes), was published in 1954, many years after the end of the Second World War. By this time, he was acutely sensitive to the ways in which nationalism had culminated in the horrors of the war, communism, and the Nazis. Nationalism, therefore, features little or not at all in his outlook, and any link between his ideas—anti-democratic to the core though they remained—and fascism or political nationalism is nonexistent. Gómez Dávila's elitist contempt for the masses and populism made him a staunch enemy of both Nazi fascism and Soviet communism. We can say, furthermore, that in his view, Nazism was the natural consequence of a disordered society, in which the rabble ultimately holds power. The project of restoring order, displaced by modernity, may have been far-fetched in the 1920s—but by the 1950s it was impossible to even entertain the fantasy. If Gómez Dávila had been born one generation earlier, he may have ended up with a radically different outlook, joining the ranks of anti-moderns like Yeats and Heidegger, who temporarily saw something promising in the fascist movements of their day. As it is, Gómez Dávila equally condemned all political solutions.

The impact of the French Catholic Revival, on the other hand, inspired Gómez Dávila much more directly and exerted a lasting influence. The movement may have had some anti-democratic tendencies, but its leaders were poets like Paul Claudel (1868–1955) and Léon Bloy (1846–1917), who were essentially apolitical. In response to the growing domination of modern rationalism and an increasing erosion of religious faith and belief, the Catholic Revivalists sought to reignite interest in what they saw as the core of Catholicism: ritual, aesthetics, and tradition. Utterly rejecting the intellectual abstractions of the scholarly theologians, the Revivalists promoted an intimate and revelatory faith. We can trace this strand directly in Gómez Dávila, for whom an intellectual understanding of God was not only unsuitable to understanding His mysteries but was fundamentally heretical—a form of self-worship in the guise of religion. The mystical union of the believer with Christ, for Gómez Dávila and the Revivalists, must be primary. Needless to say, in a process that culminated with the Second Vatican Council, the efforts of the Catholic Revival failed and the Church degenerated, over the course of Gómez Dávila's life, into a humanistic enterprise that abandons liturgies and an emphasis on the divine nature of Christ in favor of remaining "relevant," speaking to worldly or political concerns, and increasing its waning popularity. Thus, the gospel comes to be read as an ethical manual, and Christ comes to be seen as a champion for social justice rather than the incarnated God. The Revivalists can also be seen as inspirational to Gómez Dávila *because* they failed to preserve traditional Catholicism. As Jonathan Geltner writes in the introduction to his excellent new translation of Claudel's odes: "Claudel was among the last artists of the Christian civilization of western Europe: an artist who wrote from the heart of that civilization, not as an isolated survivor of it living on in an altered world."[3] Claudel, Charles Péguy (1873–1914), and the other poets of the Catholic Revival sought to keep something alive, which, during the course of Gómez Dávila's life, was to pass out of the world altogether. If, as Geltner puts it, Claudel still wrote from within the old tradition of a Christian Europe, Gómez Dávila became exactly the kind of refugee Geltner describes.

When Gómez Dávila returned to Colombia in 1932, he quickly wooed and married Emilia Nieto Ramos and settled comfortably into a routine that varied little over the next six decades of his life until his death in 1994. Aside from a trip to Europe with his wife in 1949, he never left Colombia again. In an age when travel has become a kind of mania, Gómez Dávila had little interest in seeing the world. His desire to essentially stay put may have been influenced by the observation of Thomas à Kempis (1380–1471), one of his primary spiritual guides, that "they who undertake many pilgrimages seldom become holy."[4] The world Gómez Dávila loved was not "out there," so to speak. Ernst Jünger writes that the desire for travel in the modern age is motivated by a search for something pure and untouched:

3. Claudel, *Five Great Odes*, 1.

4. Thomas à Kempis, *The Imitation of Christ* (trans. Croft and Bolton), chap. 23 ("Thoughts on Death").

> [T]oday, traveling has become a constant escape—a flight from the reality of the moment. You have to go to places where the world is not yet destroyed: it's a hunt for the ideal, a phantom.[5]

Gómez Dávila seems to have had no such compulsion. For him the "real," ideal world was the world of the imagination and the mind—the world found in his books. No external adventure could possibly compete. There is nothing in the world that we can find if it does not already exist within the self.

The vast majority of Gómez Dávila's life was spent in his library—one of the largest private libraries of any twentieth-century writer—or at the polo club, or at church, or at leisure with his family and friends. His marriage, which lasted until his death, we can assume to have been a happy one, and he had a wide circle of friends, who would frequently join him for coffee and conversation. His first book was published privately by his brother. After that, his five books were issued by obscure publishers in limited print runs. He made absolutely no attempt to expose his work to the wider public and on the few occasions that the outside world attempted to infringe on his solitude, he resolutely remained committed to quietism and withdrawal. The most notable of these incursions took place in the 1950s when Laureano Gómez, the leader of the Colombian Conservative party, urged Gómez Dávila to run for president. Needless to say, he refused.[6]

In his introduction to the German translation of Gómez Dávila's *Notas*, Martin Mosebach offers us a rare vision of the man and his home shortly before his death.[7] Regarding the Tudor-style mansion that Gómez Dávila commissioned to be built in his young adulthood on the outskirts of Bogotá, Mosebach remarks: "It is at first perplexing [to

5. Hervier, *The Details of Time*, 54.

6. Galindo Hurtado, "A Reactionary in the Andes," 3. Laureano Gómez had himself served a brief term as president of the country (1950–1951), but left office due to failing health.

7. Mosebach, "Einsiedler am Rande der bewohnten Erde," Foreword to Gómez Dávila, *Notas: Unzeitgemäße Gedanken*. All of the following Mosebach quotes are taken from this text. English translation by Michael Moynihan.

find] that Nicolás Gómez Gómez Dávila lived here, and not in Neuilly or the hills of Parioli. But then one asks oneself: Where else should a man such as this be living but on the edge of the inhabited world?" Indeed, there is something tragic in the image of a man who sought to escape from the noise and vulgarity of the modern world ending his life among the tumult of a bustling city. But this merely reinforces the fact that Gómez Dávila's withdrawal was primarily an *inner* venture. His lifelong project was to create, within himself, a sanctuary untouched by the inevitable triumph of banality, wretchedness, and degeneration. It is telling that in contrast to neighboring villas, Gómez Dávila's home was not protected by barbed wire and armed guards, but by anonymity. There is something poetically fitting about the absence of armed guards at Gómez Dávila's villa. For one who has no interest in fighting back against a society that he hates, it is preferable to simply slide into oblivion. Mosebach illustrates something of the nature of Gómez Dávila's success in creating such a sanctuary in his descriptions of the interior of the house:

> It is certainly unusual to speak about a philosophical author by describing the chambers of his home; but in the case of Nicolás Gómez Dávila it is informative, because these spaces revealed a unity of thought and life. The main hall was bare. It had a stone floor and a thick, sulfur-yellow carpet with a pattern in the center that resembled a coat of arms but was not—the family had none, despite its tradition and history that stretched back to the pre-republican period. The only wall decor was a portrait of a monk from the eighteenth century. . . . At the rear of the hall was a glass door to the courtyard where a black Buick from the 1940s was parked. Its windshield and hood were covered with a layer of yellowish dust; Barbarossa's carriage in the Kyffhäuser might have looked like this.[8] It was clear that hardly anyone ever

8. Mosebach alludes here to the folklore of the "sleeping king," which surrounds the medieval German Holy Roman Emperor Frederick Barbarossa (reigned 1155–1190). According to one well-known legend, the emperor is not dead but remains asleep with his knights inside the Kyffhäuser mountain range of Thuringia; when Germany faces its direst hour, he will emerge from the cave with his battalion to restore the nation's glory.

> sat down in the drawing room. Fancy upholstered furniture, decorated with red and silver in Colombian colonial-baroque style, was arrayed along the walls: Dávila family heirlooms from the slave-trading town of Santa Marta. In the middle of the room stood a boulle table from the Second Empire period, probably bought in Paris at the World Exposition. A blue-gray Venetian mirror dimly reflected a similarly blue-gray Spanish Madonna in the colonial-baroque style, whose vestments formed a pyramid; her small face was dark-skinned, like an Indian. The dining room was appointed with Art Deco furniture, rather austere with black lacquer and gray fabric.

Overwhelmingly, the impression created by these observations is one of tremendous gravity and stillness: in Mosebach's phrase, the interior rooms of the house felt somehow akin to "Egyptian burial chambers that would only fulfill their function after the tomb-owner's death." Interpreted another way, we might say that something great, which has passed out of the world, remained frozen there. Gómez Dávila knew better than to think that the furious pace of modernization and progress could be stopped out there in the world. And if the inner sanctum of his home was somewhat insulated against the madness out of doors, the true cloister was the one within Gómez Dávila's soul.

The portrait Mosebach paints of the man himself further intensifies the image of austerity, discipline, and profound dignity:

> The eighty-year-old Gómez Dávila, who had difficulty remaining on his feet, stood in the room as he had probably done for his entire life—slightly stooped over, as tall people tend to do who are accustomed to leaning over toward their fellow men. He was dressed in a bathrobe and clenched a cold cigar between his lips. When he greeted me, it fell to the ground, which allowed me to kneel down before him and retrieve it. Looking up, I saw a large skull with a domed forehead, *le front bombé*, like that of a statue from the late Gothic period; his cheeks looked sunken; his lips formed a thin, dark red line. With a gesture of his hand, he

> invited me into his library. He did not smile. He offered no conventional words of welcome, nor did he inquire—as one usually might—about how my journey had gone.

Now, it is important to note that Gómez Dávila at this moment was in the final year of his life and perhaps had already suffered the stroke that would eventually kill him. Mosebach writes that at this point Gómez Dávila had ceased reading, writing, or even eating, and his friends lamented that Mosebach had not met him during the prime of his life. Indeed, the sense of Gómez Dávila's character that emerges from his writing is a far cry from this rather macabre vision. We know, and shall presently see, that Gómez Dávila was a man of great humor, vivacity, and even passion. While Mosebach is not altogether wrong in feeling that he was seeing Gómez Dávila for what he truly was, even in this decrepit state—a grave shadow of a man in a cold, unheated library—his genius would certainly be less pronounced if that severity had not been tempered by those other qualities that shine forth so dramatically in his work. Mosebach's portrait of Gómez Dávila is certainly only partially accurate.

Before analyzing the content of Gómez Dávila's thought, it is important to dwell upon his preferred genre of writing. Most commonly referred to as "aphorisms," Gómez Dávila in fact wrote *scholia* or "glosses," suggesting a much more diffuse framework—simultaneously more concrete than aphorisms because they represent a form of commentary on a particular text, and more opaque because Gómez Dávila declines to tell us which texts he is commenting on, hence the titles of his books: *Glosses on an Implicit Text*, *New Glosses on an Implicit Text*, and *Successive Glosses on an Implicit Text*. Needless to say, these titles offer us nothing whatsoever and Gómez Dávila rarely refers to other authors in the glosses themselves. What we are left with, then, is a Borgesian collection of marginalia, which we can either desperately seek to attribute back to a hidden source text or, as Gómez Dávila almost certainly intended, take these comments at face value, as self-contained

Nicolás Gómez Dávila in his library.

transmissions of a *philosophia perennis*. This being said, the genre of the aphorism is clearly relevant here and there is an affinity both in style and in outlook between Gómez Dávila and figures such as François de La Rouchefoucauld (1613–1680). It is also no coincidence that Gómez Dávila has been referred to as the "Nietzsche of the Andes," a comparison that is really most accurate in terms of style rather than content. Gómez Dávila was intimately familiar with the works of Friedrich Nietzsche (1844–1900), and while there are substantive philosophical differences between the two (which we shall explore at length in what follows), the influence of the nineteenth century's most famous aphorist is abundantly evident. Gómez Dávila's glosses are sharp, incisive, and often bitterly funny. He attacks everything in modern society from politics to popular culture, to architecture, to the myopic perspective of modern science, urbanism, the plague of industrialization, and the failures of the contemporary Catholic Church. The ideas contained in these short powerful sentences are immeasurably vast and deep, and reward scrutiny and contemplation. One might sit with each gloss included in this preliminary volume for a day or more, pondering its implications and plumbing the depths of its meaning. Gómez Dávila's words offer wisdom to soothe the soul.

If referring to Gómez Dávila's glosses as marginalia illustrates something of their generic properties, however, we should not mistake them for being rushed or casual. Gómez Dávila labored intensively over the precise wording of each gloss, writing and revising until he was confident that he had succeeded in expressing something that represented a truth that was not merely the product of his own cleverness or admittedly limited intellectual power. Man's philosophy, even his own thoughts, had no value whatsoever to Gómez Dávila. Any idea that deserves to be taken seriously, in his opinion, must be one that comes from God. This is why we also see in Gómez Dávila's work, despite a degree of consistency in attitude, no attempt to formulate a totalizing worldview. Paradoxes, repetition, and contradiction are readily apparent and acknowledged—even welcomed—by the author. What can human reason do, Gómez Dávila suggests, beyond flailing helplessly in the hopes of accidently bumping up against something that exists outside of itself? Human attempts at systematic thought are invariably corrupted by the mark of their creators.

As we have noted, Gómez Dávila was bitterly hostile toward all modern political orientations and refused to identify with any of them in any way. Fascism, communism, capitalism, and democracy are attacked and dismissed with equal contempt. In this regard, he had much in common with his favorite poet, William Butler Yeats, who wrote in an unpublished letter in 1936:

> [M]y horror at the cruelty of governments grows greater, and if I did what you want I would seem to hold one form of government more responsible than any other and that would betray my convictions. Communist, fascist, nationalist,

> clerical, anticlerical are all responsible according to the number of their victims.[9]

Yeats repeated this sentiment in his final publication, *On the Boiler*, in 1938: "Republics, Kingdoms, Soviets, Corporate States, Parliaments, are trash, as Hugo said of something else 'not worth one blade of grass that God gives for the nest of the linnet.'"[10] Gómez Dávila, it seems, would have agreed entirely.

Significantly, Gómez Dávila not only used the term "reactionary" to describe himself but devoted his most powerful essay, "El reaccionario auténtico" (The Authentic Reactionary), to defining exactly what this concept meant to him. Understanding his use of the term "reactionary" is therefore vital to understanding his perspective. He eloquently summarizes the reactionary's position at the end of the essay:

> If the progressive is oriented toward the future, and the conservative toward the past, the desires of the reactionary are not based on what happened yesterday or what might happen tomorrow. The reactionary does not celebrate what the next dawn must bring, nor is he terrified by the last shadows of the night. He dwells in that luminous space where he is confronted by the eternal presence of the essential.
>
> The reactionary is liberated from the burden of history because he follows the traces of divine footsteps. For the reactionary, man and his deeds represent a slavish and mortal flesh that is merely stirred by strong winds.
>
> To be reactionary is to defend causes that do not belong to history, unconcerned that these causes are destined to lose.
>
> To be reactionary is to understand that we are only discovering what we think we are inventing; it is to admit that our imagination does not create, but rather it uncovers what has already been created and buried.
>
> To be reactionary is not to embrace certain causes, nor to advocate certain goals, but rather to submit our will to the

9. Yeats, letter to Ethel Mannin (7 April 1936), quoted in O'Brien, "Passion and Cunning," 42.

10. Yeats, *On the Boiler*, 13.

> necessity that does not constrain, to surrender our freedom to the demand that does not compel—it is to find the evidence that guides us in our sleep to the edge of ancient pools.
>
> The reactionary is not a nostalgic dreamer who yearns for the eradicated past, but rather a hunter of sacred shadows upon the eternal hills.[11]

It is clear that, like Yeats, Gómez Dávila was deeply aristocratic and elitist in his outlook. But while he fundamentally despised the masses, he also condemned the contemporary upper classes, whom he saw as uncultured, poorly educated, and thus unequipped to take any kind of leadership role in society. If the historical aristocracy was bred and trained according to hereditary ideals and principles governing their conduct, their modern counterparts were simply rich and differed from the middle class and the poor only in terms of their wealth. The bourgeois mentality thus lies at the core of Gómez Dávila's critique. In the absence of a set of virtues and values particular to each class, which confers a sense of identity, of an important place within the structure of society, money becomes the sole measure of worth. What makes Gómez Dávila's reactionary politics noteworthy, however, is that he has no interest in trying to turn back time and recognizes that any attempt to do so would be futile. This is why conservative or reactionary activism never had any appeal for him. There will be no glorious restoration. The sense of integral order that existed in society before the catastrophe of modernity is lost to us. Humanity does not determine the course of history, only God or fate or the wheel of fortune can do that. Gómez Dávila was absolutely clear about the nature of the historical moment we inhabit. Though he did not use such terms, there is no question for Gómez Dávila that this is the Kali Yuga or the Germanic *Götterdämmerung*.

The properly reactionary position, in Gómez Dávila's assessment, is characterized by an awareness that there is no direction or meaning to history. Progress—whether as conceived of by the secular humanist or the liberal Catholic—is a myth. We are moving neither forward to a future utopia nor backward to a past Golden Age. Following Spengler,

11. Gómez Dávila, "El reaccionario auténtico," 19. Translation by Ramon Elani and Michael Moynihan, with thanks to Dr. Pedro Ortega for his helpful clarifications.

we are merely repeating the same cyclical patterns, which change only in their outward forms and circumstances. The same eternal truths, those which derive from the divine and exist outside of time or historical contingency, are perpetually recoverable, at least within the soul of the individual. Recoverable, that is, so long as we orient ourselves not toward the tumult and chaos of our present concerns. In the words of Novalis: "Only that is true which has occurred at no time and in no place."[12] For Gómez Dávila, therefore, the reactionary is one who studies history in order to try to perceive, amidst the chaos, disorder, and ruin, those traces of divine wisdom that may guide us through endless cycles. The progressive and the conservative are alike in believing that they may direct history, and both refuse to acknowledge that humanity is enslaved to history. The reactionary refuses to try to direct the course of history and clings to whatever scraps of wisdom and dignity he may accumulate and preserve. This perennial wisdom, however, is just as likely to be lost or forgotten as it is to be recovered. So humanity is doomed to forever oscillate between understanding and ignorance.

If Gómez Dávila's sense of history is largely determined by his religious faith, we must also attempt to situate his unique understanding of Christianity. To say that Gómez Dávila was a devout Catholic is accurate but insufficient. In fact, there may be little in his vision that is familiar to most Catholics, especially today. For example, the majority of contemporary Catholics are unlikely to find democracy or even liberalism incompatible with their faith. Even further, however, while Gómez Dávila was intimately familiar with the writings of Augustine and Thomas à Kempis and was influenced by them, the nature of his faith is ultimately hostile to theology. As we have said above, following Claudel, Gómez Dávila's faith was a personal and existential one. He went to mass regularly but paid little attention to sermons, which he felt actually undermined proper faith. A God who is the product of rational thought, he believed, does not deserve to be worshiped. The true value of the Church, in Gómez Dávila's eyes, was in preserving ritual and tradition. To cast aside antiquated liturgies, therefore, was heretical. To bring Catholicism into the realm of worldly or political concerns was heretical. The incense, the music, the architecture, and

12. Quoted in Hervier, *The Details of Time*, 93.

the symbolism of the historical Catholic Church was vital because it marked that space as fundamentally *separate*, as outside the world, and even as a counterforce to the world. But perhaps the most significant factor that requires us to view Gómez Dávila's Catholicism as something other than orthodox is his attitude toward paganism.

In his own intriguingly mysterious words, Gómez Dávila described himself as a "pagan who believes in Christ."[13] What are we to make of this formulation? As a Catholic, Gómez Dávila certainly believed that Christianity had the greatest claim to divine wisdom, but it seems that he did not believe its claim was exclusive. Indeed, given the ways the Second Vatican Council shifted so much of the Church's emphasis away from the divine and toward the human realm, Gómez Dávila may have been increasingly willing to accept non-Christian paths toward the attainment of perennial wisdom. If the modern Catholic Church abandons its role as preserver of tradition, it only stands to reason that one might look elsewhere. But just as Gómez Dávila sought to stay loyal to the antiquated aristocratic ideas of virtue and dignity internally, even as those ideas vanished from the outside world, it may be that he quietly resolved the problems of the modern Church within his soul. Nevertheless, it appears that Gómez Dávila was uniquely prepared to accept the validity of traditional wisdom wherever he found it. As Alain de Benoist observes in *On Being a Pagan*, any religion is better than no religion at all.[14] Gómez Dávila would have certainly agreed. As the secular worldview continues to expand its influence in modern society, all those who affirm the divine nature of man and the world must certainly be on the same side.

So, if modern society has abandoned God and religion—whence does it derive its authority and sense of meaning? For Gómez Dávila, the answer was clear: modern humanity, beginning with the *philosophes* of the Enlightenment, worships only itself. Capitalism, democracy, and industrialism, for Gómez Dávila, all stem from this fundamental heresy. In passing, we might observe that perhaps Heidegger, in attributing the source of the modern disease to the age of Plato, may have been closer to the mark. After all, Protagoras's formulation

13. Gómez Dávila, *Escolios a un Texto Implícito: Selección*, 113.

14. Benoist, *On Being a Pagan* (trans. Graham), vi: "Of course not all beliefs are equal, but there is one thing worse than a vile belief and that is the total absence of faith."

"Man is the measure of all things" significantly predates the French Revolution. Even so, the fact remains that only in the past three or four hundred years—with the advent of modern technology—has it been possible for humanity to entertain the delusion that it is the sole agent in the cosmos. The act of placing humanity at the center of the universe is the ultimate expression of profanity, from which all other modern ills emanate. These include the scientific vision, which suggests that reality is capable of being perceived through human intellection alone; and democracy, which suggests that society can be organized correctly according to human reason.

As we shall see, Gómez Dávila also anticipated some of the themes of contemporary ecology, which has contentiously suggested that our current geological age may be termed the "Anthropocene," as it is defined by mankind's disruption of biospherical systems. Industrialism and ecological collapse was, for him, an inescapable consequence of humanism. A mankind that views itself as the center of the world in cosmological or spiritual terms is much more likely to view nonhuman lives—or the biosphere as a whole—as secondary concerns. If human reason is assumed to be the source of all meaning, we should not be surprised to find that nature only has value as it relates to humanity. A humanistic perspective is only capable of viewing nature as material for the betterment of humanity. Even in its most enlightened form, humanism laments the loss of biodiversity and environmental health only insofar as it impacts human life and well-being. Humanism simply cannot articulate an argument in favor of the inherent value of nature. For Gómez Dávila, who saw firsthand the devastating ecological consequences of industrialism around his childhood home, the tragic destruction of nature was an abiding concern because the natural world is divine. Without such a sacred view of the world, anything nonhuman must be passive, lacking agency, and insignificant.

Among the other byproducts of humanism, some of which we have already discussed, the critique of technology appears over and over again in Gómez Dávila's writing. Technology, for Gómez Dávila, presumes to put enormous power into human hands but only succeeds in degrading us. He utterly denied technology's ability to meaningfully improve human life and primarily describes it in his work as either an instrument of destruction or as a vehicle for stupidity and laziness.

But Gómez Dávila was no self-righteous purist. He does not exempt himself from his condemnation of the modern world. In denouncing the evils of technology, he does not presume to advocate the position of an idealistic luddite. While Gómez Dávila's lifestyle may have been "old fashioned" or eccentric, he certainly did not try to run away from technological society and live in an off-the-grid cabin à la Ted Kaczynski. This would have violated Gómez Dávila's belief that there are *no* solutions to the problems of the world. We cannot run away from the modern world; we cannot create a different kind of world within this one; we cannot defeat the modern world through sabotage, terrorism, or any kind of political shuffling. Here we return to Gómez Dávila's notion of an inner retreat, which is decidedly not a solution, as hysterical activists are so keen to remind us. But Gómez Dávila would have agreed with the do-gooders that withdrawal is fundamentally a defeatist position. The authentic reactionary, for Gómez Dávila, does not try to "win"—because to do so in this world would necessarily require him to abandon the very principles he is fighting for. There is grace, honor, dignity, and even wisdom in defeat. Liberals, socialists, anarchists, communists, fascists, and conservatives all want to "win" so that they can make the world look more like what they want it to look like. The reactionary, the authentic reactionary, on the other hand, is content to remain loyal to his principles and to despise what he sees without thinking there is anything he can do to change it.

Unsurprisingly, Gómez Dávila's critique of technology is nuanced and subtle. Evoking the distinction between tools and machines, he notes the massive discrepancy between those who create or design machines and those who use them. While the creation of machines requires an enormous degree of technical skill and knowledge, they can be fully operated by a person of the meanest possible intelligence. The fact that such powerful technology is put into the hands of the general public is part of Gómez Dávila's hostility toward it. Technology would be much less dangerous if it was harder to use or required a greater degree of intelligence and judgment. As a matter of fact, we might say that in general technology has a democratizing effect. If the printing press began the process of allowing the foolish, cruel, and ignorant to broadcast their darkest, most wretched thoughts and opinions far and wide, the Internet and telecommunications technology has led us to the point where one is quite literally surrounded by repugnant, idiotic ideas twenty-four hours a day, whether we want to hear them or not. What does technology really do, Gómez Dávila begs us to ask, other than embolden and encourage stupidity and ignorance? The contemporary imbecile of the modern world has an almost inconceivable amount of power at his fingertips.

In one of his more poignant glosses, Gómez Dávila notes that technology really does nothing but increase our power to kill and destroy. Does technology make humanity healthier or happier? Does it teach us how to love? Does it make us wiser? Does it strengthen our communities? Does it bring us closer to God? Advances in medicine—often touted as the greatest justification for unbridled technology—make human beings live longer, even as their lives become increasingly empty, boring, and miserable. Ernst Jünger observes in conversation with Julien Hervier:

> Monstrous energies come to us, and what do we do with them? Instead of building a magnificent world and great utopias where, for instance, no one would have to work—we don't even consider it, we use our [Aladdin's] lamp to stockpile nuclear bombs.[15]

Broadly speaking, we might say that the anti-democratic position is characterized as misanthropic or cruel. In other words, it is assumed that the reactionary is motivated by a hatred of the masses or even of humanity as a whole. While Gómez Dávila does not try to disguise his hatred for many aspects of modern life and modern humanity, it would be a mistake to think that his contempt and disdain constitutes an unconditional hatred for humanity or even the so-called rabble. In fact, as we shall see below, he explicitly states that aristocratic societies of the past had value *primarily* because of how they allowed the common man to flourish and live an honorable, meaningful life. Marxist historians may bristle at this, but the fact remains that Gómez Dávila genuinely believed that the medieval peasant lived with more dignity and purpose than the billions of wage slaves under modern liberal capitalism. And as it turns out, some contemporary analyses of

15. Hervier, *The Details of Time*, 117.

the working conditions of serfs conclude that they had a much greater degree of freedom than the workers of today. As Galindo Hurtado notes:

> [T]he reactionary, contrary to a well spread belief, criticises with such fury the modern world not because he hates it, but because he loves too much the conditions that, in his own mind of course, have made the greatness of it. He wants the best possible of worlds, and will accept nothing short of that. Convinced that human life depends on a delicate balance between order and freedom to prosper and exude its best qualities, he is ready to defend those conditions that in the past allowed for the blossoming of the spirit in all its magnificence.[16]

While liberty is an enormously contested term even within Gómez Dávila's work, we may say that he believed aristocratic societies were infinitely better equipped to promote and defend liberty than modern democracy. If the aristocratic ideal is greatness, the democratic ideal is mediocrity. Needless to say, this benefits the common man as little as it benefits the so-called elite. As the pioneering reactionary feminist Mary Harrington observes, given the fact that violence against women is overwhelmingly committed by men, one would think it would be in women's interest for men to have a code of conduct that teaches them to treat women with courtesy and gentleness. The vanishing of chivalry harms women as much or more than it harms men. So, too, with the other aristocratic values and principles. The passing of the old feudal order leaves us all at the mercy of each other.

While we know that peasant uprisings were common in medieval life, Gómez Dávila believed that the rigid social boundaries of feudalism actually limited the conditions for class struggle. If leadership in society is conferred through birth and training rather than merely the acquisition of material wealth, and there is no mechanism in society for movement between classes, Gómez Dávila argued that people, regardless of their class, would be more content with their lot in life. In the absence of meaningful class distinctions and in societies where

16. Galindo Hurtado, "A Reactionary in the Andes," 11.

money is the only source of power, the lower classes will necessarily desire to raise themselves above their condition. This gets to the core of pernicious ideas such as the "American Dream," which teaches us that if we work hard enough and generate enough wealth, we can live better lives. The current realities of capitalist society provide ample evidence to disprove this fantasy. Beyond a minute number of exceptions, the poor will never be able to work hard enough to compete against the advantages of the rich. Social mobility, in other words, is a myth, which only serves to increase resentment and envy. The feudal commoner was not less poor than the modern capitalist worker, but he did not break his body and torture his soul in thinking that he could become something more than what he was. The aristocratic society, for Gómez Dávila, is one in which all members of society accept their place and perform their duties. And this acceptance and sense of duty provide a legitimate source of worth and pride. Georges Dumézil, in his analysis of the tripartite structure of Indo-European societies, gives us a way to understand this dynamic. Society cannot exist without kings and lawgivers, but it also cannot exist without providers. Democratic society teaches people that they should all be kings, thereby denigrating the role of the provider and radically misunderstanding the role of the king.

Gómez Dávila reminds us that the monarchs and aristocrats of the past hardly enjoyed the absolute freedom imagined by progressives and democrats. The aristocracy was *bound* by a no less restrictive system of life and conduct than that which governed the peasantry—the explicit prohibition against commercial activity, for example. The aristocrat was born and bred, through rigorous training passed down through generations, to govern and rule. He was expected to diligently perform this duty, which made enormous demands upon his time and energy. It is a fallacy of the modern democratic position that most or all men desire power or are capable of wielding that power. The truth is that most people would rather spend their days working at their simple jobs and then coming home and watching a football game. The crowning glory of the aristocratic system is that it recognizes and validates nonproductive and non-financial goals. This is true both for the commoner who spends his considerable leisure time celebrating festivals, drinking, and socializing, and the aristocrat whose obligations include the cultivation of artistic talent and sporting.

We may say that, ultimately, Gómez Dávila's rejection of democracy stemmed from his distrust of reason, which he shares with many other important reactionary thinkers such as Edmund Burke (1729–1797) and Joseph de Maistre (1753–1821). Politics, as is increasingly clear in our own historical moment, is not rational but libidinal. Voters do not respond to reason, intelligent considerations, or measured analysis, but to fears, passions, intuitions, and prejudices. Without the guidance of an educated and trained elite, who subscribe to a set of high-minded ideals and principles, society is inevitably torn apart by ignorance, partisan concerns, hysteria, and paranoia, or as Yeats put it in *The Second Coming*: "mere anarchy."[17] The masses do not act according to reason and, thus, by putting political power in their hands, society itself becomes insane. Here we can also see why Gómez Dávila has no faith in the modern elites, who are poorly educated and are possessed by the same vulgar bourgeois values as everybody else.

Having established a number of themes that broadly characterize Gómez Dávila's thought, we must now turn to the matter of his influences and his library, a vital consideration for an author who almost exclusively presented his work as glosses or commentary, as we have described above. Till Kinzel's fine essay "Aphoristic Thought, the Problem of Reading and the 'Implicit Library': Reflections on Nicolás Gómez Dávila" does much to illuminate the subject. Kinzel, who is perhaps the world's foremost scholar of Gómez Dávila, begins by gesturing toward Nietzsche, who argued in favor of "a kind of reading that is the product of leisure, of *schole* in the Greek sense."[18] This style of reading, which is primarily "digestive, repetitive and meditative" is, in and of itself, a challenge to the modern mentality and largely alien to modern readers, maybe most of all to professional scholars or academics, whose genuine desire to engage in such reading is likely to be interrupted and discouraged by the demands of their job.

Gómez Dávila's stated intention to have written a "concentric book" rather than a linear one demonstrates how his work should be read. Since he is generally circling around the same ideas and authors,

17. Yeats, *The Collected Poems*, 187.

18. Kinzel, "Aphoristic Thought, the Problem of Reading and the 'Implicit Library,'" 22.

trying to get ever closer to the timeless germ of wisdom contained therein, there is a necessary amount of repetition. His scholia, constantly referring back to the enormity of the implicit text, carry a density and weight masked by their brevity. Nevertheless, the experience of reading Gómez Dávila resembles less that of the investigator or textual analyst and more the explorer or mountain climber. Kinzel writes: "The aphorisms of Gómez Dávila seem to project like individual mountain tops from the great and undefinable virtual space of the implicit library or, to say it metaphorically, they represent tiny peep-holes through which one can view parts of the implicit library."[19] Indeed, while the analyst or scholar will find in the scholia an insufficient amount of data to draw his measured conclusions, the adventurer must simply steel his nerves and have the courage to confront his fears. Reading Gómez Dávila rewards the brave.

Given Gómez Dávila's enormous debt to Michel de Montaigne (1533–1592), which we will describe more in depth below, it is no surprise that he models his own method of both reading and writing on the man whom Kinzel calls Gómez Dávila's "patron saint." Montaigne's reading of classical authors, as he himself admits, though extensive, is unsystematic. He dips in and out of Seneca or Plutarch at will, and stubbornly refuses to properly attribute the quotations he deploys. The motivation for this eccentric practice is revealed in a sentence from Montaigne's essay "Of Books," which Gómez Dávila cites in his final volume of scholia: "I want them to give Plutarch a filip on my nose and get burned insulting Seneca in me."[20] Thus, Montaigne essentially allows himself to stand in for his favorite authors, encouraging his readers to conflate them. This methodology is taken to the extreme by Gómez Dávila, who refuses to even name his sources in his own work. In fact, as we shall see, he specifically tried to integrate the ideas of others to the extent that their influence is dimly perceived but never directly felt or seen. A lesser thinker, Gómez Dávila states, depends on constantly referencing others. A true intellect incorporates them to the point that it is impossible to distinguish between where his thought ends and the thought of the other begins. Nevertheless, we shall try to

19. Kinzel, "Aphoristic Thought," 26.

20. Montaigne, *The Complete Works* (trans. Frame), 296–97.

trace some of these influences here. And this will not be the last, nor the most blasphemous, perversion of Gómez Dávila's intentions in this present work.

Since Gómez Dávila largely refuses to acknowledge his debts to other thinkers, much is left for us to piece together. Luckily, we know what books he owned and can gather some details from that. We can draw certain limited conclusions from the fact, for example, that Gómez Dávila owned a complete set of the works of G. K. Chesterton (1874–1936) but only a single volume of Julius Evola (1898–1974). Likewise, the presence of a number of secondary volumes on certain authors indicates sustained study and interest. Such is the case with Nietzsche. Then, of course, with sufficient patience and discernment, we can detect the presence of others in his words, standing behind him like a multitude of ghosts. My attempts to do so here will be radically incomplete. A fully annotated edition of Gómez Dávila may someday appear and do much to contribute to a more thorough understanding of his philosophy. Here we merely seek to gesture and create an impression.

It may be beneficial to identify a number of the authors whose works are heavily represented in Gómez Dávila's library. Complete or nearly complete collections include D. H. Lawrence, Jacob Burckhardt, Carl Jung, G. K. Chesterton, Ludwig Klages, Joseph de Maistre, Edmund Burke, Thomas Carlyle, John Ruskin, Hillaire Belloc, W. B. Yeats, Alexis de Tocqueville, Christopher Dawson, Georges Dumézil, Ernst Jünger, T. S Eliot, Martin Heidegger, Oswald Spengler, Michel de Montaigne, Johann Wolfgang von Goethe, Friedrich Nietzsche, and Karl Marx. Added to this, of course, is a wide range of classical authors. Subjects and themes well represented in Gómez Dávila's library include ancient and modern history, philosophy, prehistoric culture, mythology, Eastern thought and culture, and philology. Gómez Dávila read English, Latin, French, and German with great facility. Some notable omissions are just as illustrative. Gómez Dávila possessed very few works by the twentieth-century traditionalists; for example, Julius Evola, René Guénon, and Frithjof Schuon are hardly represented at all. This we might simply attribute to the fact that Gómez Dávila preferred the spiritual traditions of the West over the East. But we might also recall that even Guénon believed that

Catholicism might be the most suitable path for Europeans to connect with the *sophia perennis*. There are no volumes on fascism whatsoever in Gómez Dávila's library, suggesting perhaps how little of worth he found there. On the other hand, the works of Karl Marx and other Marxist thinkers are very well represented, despite his overwhelming hostility toward Marxism as a political ideology. Nearly all the great representatives of the high Victorian novel are present in his library, and one can easily picture the comforting image of Gómez Dávila, wrapped in a blanket, smoking a cigar, reading Dickens or Anthony Trollope.

In terms of the few direct references and explicit engagements with other writers that are present in Gómez Dávila, we might dwell chiefly on two examples: Nietzsche and Montaigne. The latter, as we have seen, presented Gómez Dávila with a style of reading and writing that constitutes a deep engagement with others, while obscuring the precise nature of that engagement, thus placing the onus on the reader to reflect, reread, and puzzle over. Nietzsche, on the other hand, often appears in Gómez Dávila as a foil.

In the case of Montaigne, we can easily perceive a number of direct influences: his deep affinity for the wisdom of the classics, his realist or stoic perspective, his committed devotion to discovering what is timeless and eternal amidst the flux of history, and his insistence upon authentically presenting to the reader the truth of his own soul. Needless to say, however, Gómez Dávila did not share Montaigne's skeptical attitude toward religion and his emphasis on secular free thinking.

We might think that Nietzsche's aristocratic philosophy, valorization of ancient virtue, and contempt for the modern world would make him a natural complement to Gómez Dávila, but on closer examination the two may be more accurately described as opposites. The revolutionary romantic position, which makes triumphant heroes of oppressed figures such as Prometheus and Lucifer, could not be further from Gómez Dávila. The hero, the man of will, who stands alone against the very order of the cosmos itself, becomes, for Gómez Dávila, the ideal representative of the modern delusion. Nietzsche's declaration of the death of God, for example, is a joke to Gómez Dávila. The very essence of the modern disease, for Gómez Dávila, is the deification of mankind suggested by the Nietzschean *Übermensch*.

In closing, a few words on Gómez Dávila's possible reception in today's society are needed. In the West we are currently witnessing an increasing sense of disillusionment with established political and historical narratives. Francis Fukuyama's belief in the triumph of liberal, capitalist, democratic values appears to be shared by fewer and fewer people. Added to this general dissatisfaction with the status quo, we can see evidence of a political realignment. What has been assumed to be the domain of the left wing for the last several decades is increasingly appearing in right-wing spaces. Issues of free speech and the role of law enforcement in the United States have been repositioned following the Covid crisis and the Trumpist so-called insurrection attempt at the Capitol. In this confused ideological climate, some strand of reactionary thought, which *might* accord with Gómez Dávila's definition, is emerging. Since the conservative position depends on the idea that there still exists something in contemporary society that is valid and true—which is an increasingly difficult argument to make—more and more on the Right are abandoning conventional Republican values. Of course, the vast majority of these are unfortunately drawn instead to the new brand of populist nationalism, which is currently enjoying much success in the United States, Italy, Hungary, and elsewhere in the West. But a number of contemporary thinkers are walking away from both the Left and the Right, and beginning to speak in terms that start to sound a little like Gómez Dávila.

In his 2021 book *The Reactionary Mind: Why "Conservative" Isn't Enough*, the conservative Catholic author Michael Warren Davis presents a highly accessible overview of the reactionary position. In this volume, clearly written for a popular audience, Davis approvingly cites sources as diverse as the late leftist anthropologist David Graeber, G. K. Chesterton, democratic senator Elizabeth Warren, and the localist agrarian philosopher Wendell Berry. One finds in Davis's book a rejection of both capitalism and socialism, Democrat and Republican partisan politics, big tech, urbanism, progressivism, and many other features of modern society. In their place, he proposes the figure of the reactionary, who

> rejects the cheapness, the artificiality, of modern life. He demands the right to pursue his own happiness, and he refuses to accept mere comfort instead. He doesn't want to survive; he wants to live. And he wants to go to heaven.[21]

Davis ends his book by advocating a number of steps one can take toward achieving these goals, including starting a family, homeschooling, reading, creating local community, moving to the country, farming, avoiding technology, abstaining from voting or participation in national politics, and daily prayer. He closes with a quote from Anthony Burgess: "I suppose my conservatism, since the idea of a Catholic Jacobite imperial monarch isn't practical, is really a kind of anarchism."[22] Gómez Dávila likely would have largely approved of this sentiment. Retreat or withdrawal will not be a compelling call to arms for many, but there seems to be a dawning recognition that things are not going to get better and therefore looking inward might be the last best option remaining to us. In this, however, Gómez Dávila departs from the stoic philosophers and Heidegger's *Gelassenheit* or "acceptance." Withdrawal from modern society is incomplete if it is not accompanied by a contemptuous indictment and condemnation. Like Yeats, Gómez Dávila's position was primarily antithetical, rejecting everything and proposing nothing.

21. Davis, *The Reactionary Mind*, 195.

22. Davis, *The Reactionary Mind*, 203.

Ramon Elani

A Note on the Translations and Commentaries

Nicolás Gómez Dávila labored over the precise wording of his scholia. The more an author brutalizes his words, he believed, the kinder he was to his readers. I have taken this sentiment at face value and often brutalized Gómez Dávila's words in order to translate them into what is hopefully clear and elegant English. There are times when I have been able to let the simplicity of Gómez Dávila's language come through with minimal alterations. There are also occasions when I have entirely departed from his language in order to grasp the essential spirit of his words. While this kind of deviation is accepted practice in translation, scholars of Gómez Dávila may, with good reason, raise their eyebrows at my decision to provide commentary.

In the matter of commentary, I have perhaps blasphemously undermined Gómez Dávila's entire project. What the reader will find here is—scandalously!—commentary piled on top of commentary. While Gómez Dávila precisely condensed the contents of his implicit library, I have violated that spirit of brevity with my own reflections and references. Occasionally, I have even gone so far as to commit the cardinal sin of unmasking those implicit sources that populate Gómez Dávila's writing. Where Gómez Dávila's project has been to make small what is big, I have perversely attempted to make the small big again. I have to believe, on some level, however, that the reader will understand what I am trying to do here. Contraction and expansion are complementary forces. Just as history follows a sequence of cyclical growth and degeneration, I believe that Gómez Dávila's work, the product of radical contraction, tantalizes us with the promise of expansion. The processes of reflection and inspiration, which are ultimately expansive in character, are the natural consequence of reading. I do not expect or intend that my commentary will replace the readers' own internal responses to Gómez Dávila's words. I have included them rather as a document of *this* reader's journey through the mind of this brilliant man and presented them as a model for how every other reader may progress on his own journey. If Gómez Dávila succeeded in writing a concentric book, I have merely hoped to widen that circle.

A few further words are in order regarding the polemical tone of my commentaries. The tenderhearted reader may have cause to bristle and demand to know: *to whom* am I referring when I speak broadly of "modern man"? To which I shall respond in the words of Swinburne's "pale Galilean" that "None are without sin. No, not one." The truth is that it does not much matter whether one group or another is more (or less) to blame for the present state of things and—more tragically still—none are exempt from the consequences of modernity. Industrial chemicals are present in the smallest animal drifting about senselessly at the bottom of the Mariana Trench. No group is immune or without blame: not Christians, not the unvaccinated, not the indigenous, not social-justice activists, not pagan revivalists, not organic farmers, not spiritual seekers who have been initiated in unbroken traditions of ancient wisdom, not anti-racists, not Third-Worldists or anti-Americans, not anarchists. This is the Kali Yuga. This is a *universal* condition. This is the point at which the earth has drifted to the furthest distance from the cosmic center.

The fact that it is all too easy to identify, in retrospect, how we got to this stage should not tempt us into thinking it could have been avoided. It is not a coincidence or a careless bit of clumsy prose that I frequently give agency to this thing that I have labeled "modernity." The wheel of fortune turns, and the fate of the world rises and falls accordingly. Our blessing and our curse is in recognizing how little we have to do with any of it. Yes, man has made a wreckage of this world. But when has he properly understood the motives or the consequences of his own actions? He is a blind fool stumbling about in the dark. The hand of man is guided by fate or the will of the gods. The Eddas and the Puranas do not tell us that the end of the world has come because man has strayed from the path of virtue, but rather that man has strayed from the path of virtue because it is the end of the world.

Even among those who essentially understand the depth of the crisis that faces us, there is a tendency to assume that if one is clever enough, or pure enough, or enlightened enough, one will be spared and act as a shining beacon for those poor lost souls who just weren't spiritually or materially prepared. The early twentieth-century Traditionalists believed that they could be an ark or repository for the true wisdom of humanity, which could be used to reconstruct the *sophia perennis* among the ruins. But while two figures (whose names,

Líf and Lífþrasir, mean "Life" and "Eager-for-Life") may emerge from the cataclysm of Ragnarok, there is no reason to assume that this refers to a chosen group of the elect. It merely reminds us that after the conflagration which awaits us at the close of our present twilight age, "the new yet ever-ancient sun will break through the horror; thunder will only roll on the faraway mountains; the white dove will soar aloft in the blue skies; and the Earth, weeping, will rise like a liberated beauty in new glory" (Eichendorff, *Ahnung und Gegenwart*, 291–92).

Source citations: There are several authors whose work is quoted from regularly in the commentaries. The parenthetical citations that appear after these quotes refer to page numbers—or, in the case of Nietzsche, aphorism numbers—in the following editions (see Works Cited section for complete bibliographic details):

Jacob Burckhardt: *Judgments on History and Historians*, translated by Harry Zohn.

G. K. Chesterton: *Orthodoxy*.

Paul Claudel: *Five Great Odes*, translated by Jonathan Geltner.

Ernst Jünger: Julien Hervier, *The Details of Time: Conversation with Jünger*, translated by Joachim Neugroschel.

Joseph de Maistre: *Major Works*, vol. 1, translated by Edward Maxwell III.

Michel de Montaigne: *Essays*, translated by J. M. Cohen.

Friedrich Nietzsche: *Beyond Good and Evil*, translated by R. J. Hollingdale and *Twilight of the Idols* and *The Anti-Christ*, translated by R. J. Hollingdale.

Oswald Spengler: *The Decline of the West: An Abridged Edition*, translated by Charles Francis Atkinson; edited by Helmut Werner.

N.B.: For those who may wish to read these scholia in the original, a bracketed reference appears at the end of each commentary—[*ETIS* 215], for example—which provides a page number for the scholium in the edition *Escolios a un Texto Implícito: Selección* (Bogotá: Villegas, 2005).

Acknowledgments: This book, which began as an idle fantasy, was brought to life through the keen editorial acumen and vision of Michael Moynihan and Joshua Buckley; the expert assistance of Dr. Till Kinzel; and the support and patience of my wife and children, among whom at least Nicolás Gómez Dávila has become a household name. I hope to have done honor to the memory of this remarkable man.

I
History

1. **History demonstrates not the inefficacy of actions, but rather the futility of intentions.**

It is a common mistake to assume that the quietist or reactionary believes that action is useless. In fact, we believe that action is much worse than useless. What history shows time and time again is that humanity is incapable of understanding the consequences of its actions. Action can certainly bring about change. But what will that change look like? Humanity has frequently acted with vigor and with the best possible intentions. And yet, predictably, the fruits of those actions lead to disaster and suffering. The most glorious revolution will always lead to terror. Any child who has absorbed the traditional wisdom found in folktales instinctively knows this to be the case. The best-laid plans often go astray; count no man lucky until he is dead. [*ETIS* 37]

2. **History buries its problems without resolving them.**

In the realm of human action, there is little evidence that problems can be solved. This does not mean, however, that certain problems do not temporarily cease to plague us. We just confuse their coming and going with our ability to direct the course of events. Historical causes are many and varied, and inevitably lie beyond our capacity for reason and understanding. Humanity pores over history, searching for explanations. But the mass graves of history are largely unmarked and nobody can say who died there or what was achieved by their deaths. When we exhume the dead and seek to give them justice after their time, we accomplish nothing more than disturbing their rest and our own blissful forgetfulness. One might say that history demonstrates the ongoing inability to resist plundering the tombs of the dead and an infinitely repeating sequence of curses from beyond the grave. If it is clear that history presents no solutions and that even an understanding of history is doomed to failure, the best we can do is witness, record, and provide a standard by which history may be judged. For Gómez Dávila, this was the triumph of the Catholic Church. [*ETIS* 32]

3. **Two hundred years ago one could trust in the future without being totally stupid. Today who can believe in the current prophecies, since we are living in the splendid future of yesterday?**

We can forgive the blind optimism of the utopian idealists of the early modern period. There was good reason for them to suppose that history was progressing. They saw the emergence of innovations that would revolutionize human life and thought. They were not fools to think that the next day would be better than the one before. But—and we cannot possibly overstate this fact—they were wrong. We can excuse their optimism even while acknowledging that it was hopelessly misguided. Our world, the world of the twenty-first century, was meant to be their paradise. We have seen their dream of liberation through democracy turn into a political system utterly dominated by wealth and exploited by populist demagogues. We have seen their dream of technology become the means of poisoning and degrading the human body and soul. We have seen their dream of industrialization turn nature into a barren wasteland. When we see all this, when we see what has become of the utopian visions of yesterday, how can anyone trust in the optimists of today? [*ETIS* 59]

4. **Intelligence isolates; stupidity congregates.**

Stupidity loves company, while intelligence flourishes in solitude. Intelligence provokes envy and resentment, while stupidity comforts and ingratiates. Intelligence challenges and distinguishes, while stupidity is agreeable and easy to please. The intelligent man will always be alone and treated by his fellows with suspicion at best—and outright hostility at worst. The stupid man will be universally adored and welcomed with open arms wherever he appears. How often have history's wisest, most brilliant minds been despised and condemned? The ignorant masses, on the other hand, never lose. Any cause can win by appealing to stupidity, which is the great leveler. [*ETIS* 387]

5. **History is irreversible.**
But it is not unrepeatable.

The wheel of history may only turn in one direction, but it always keeps turning. Eventually, the wheel will come back around. As Ernst Jünger puts it:

> If we believe, or accept the hypothesis, that a cyclical order exists, this hypothesis goes beyond the notion of progress. Progress is linear, while cyclical movements return to their starting points. (63)

What does this returning motion suggest? Spengler, who received his methodology of understanding world history as living nature from Goethe, writes: "Every thought, faith and science dies as soon as the spirits in whose worlds their 'eternal truths' were true and necessary are extinguished" (90). Cultures calcify into civilizations and pass out of history, never to return. And yet, cultures, as organic forms, continue to bubble up like some kind of fungoid growth, and are destined to repeat the same sequence of evolution. "There is," Spengler reminds us, "a wondrous music of the spheres which wills to be heard and which a few of our deepest spirits will hear" (86). Specific forms vanish forever, but the same sequences repeat themselves over and over again. [*ETIS* 258]

6. **Clarity is the reward of the vanquished.**

In the clear, harsh light of defeat, dispelled of our giddy illusions, we perceive things as they truly are. The same cannot be said for the victor, who is only too happy to rewrite the past. Indeed, the winner is obligated to lie in order to validate his actions, and in time he even forgets why he fought and the cost of his victory. But the defeated man never forgets. If he is deprived of the spoils, what he preserves may be even more valuable. A vanquished truth is worth far more than a triumphant lie. [*ETIS* 303]

7. **The vanishing of the peasantry and the classical humanities severed the continuity with the past.**

When reading, as Montaigne did, the works of antiquity, one is shocked by how contemporary their concerns seem. And in the face of such familiar considerations, the wisdom of the classics both articulates a fundamental truth and enacts it, to wit, that there is nothing new. The only recourse for the true seeker of knowledge is to attempt to reconstruct within himself that which has already been learned and then forgotten by countless successive prior generations.

The modern, as we know, has a mania for novelty. As Chesterton puts it:

> All the towering materialism which dominates the modern mind rests ultimately upon one assumption; a false assumption. It is supposed that if a thing goes on repeating

itself it is probably dead; a piece of clockwork. (60)

The vibrancy and meaning of life is not experienced in the compulsive desire for the new, but in repetition and routine. The historical peasant or the rural man of today is intimately acquainted with the value of repetition. For one who is tied to the land, novelty carries little charm. If something is good and important in and of itself, then it stands to reason that we should want to do it again and again, with as little variation as possible. The wisdom of the classics is not diminished by the fact that we have heard it all before. That is precisely the nature of its genius. [*ETIS* 351]

8. **Mankind never accounts for the cost of any commodity it has gained by conquest.**

As Spengler and Montaigne keenly observed, the enormous wealth that poured into Europe during the sixteenth century was acquired through the annihilation of the greatest civilizations of the New World. Whatever was gained by it pales in comparison to what had been lost. Man reckons wealth gained in this manner to be found money, a windfall. But debts will always be paid. Could industrialism have developed without this unprecedented influx of resources? Could the modern state? Did not the conquest of the New World begin the moment that the feudal order began to collapse? If the modern world itself was born out of the sin of colonialism, then Moctezuma and the Capacs have surely had their revenge many times over. [*ETIS* 444]

9. **Earth will never be a paradise, but it might be possible to avoid turning it into a cheap imitation of hell.**

There might be limits to how happy and peaceful humanity can be, but there are no limits to how miserable and evil we can be. Therefore, if things can never be perfect, we can at least try not to make them so horrible. Much of human history seems to have existed in some sort of balance, given the previous limits of man's ability to rely exclusively upon his own resources. If we abandon the project of creating an ideal utopian world, we can still attempt to avoid creating a boring and tedious nightmare. But even this, now, seems to be too much to ask. [*ETIS* 378]

10. **The West withers every non-Western soul that encounters it.**

The tragic fate of the great Meso-American and South American civilizations at the hands of the conquistadors, which so disturbed thinkers like Montaigne in the sixteenth century, is one that has been shared by the entire world in the twenty-first century. To speak of the globalization of the world is the same as to speak of the modernization of the world or the Westernization of the world. Of course, we would not think to suggest that it would have been otherwise had circumstances favored the East. It has even been argued by Bengali novelist Amitav Ghosh that the ravages of Western colonialism in India and China kept those civilizations from modernizing and industrializing a century earlier. As Spengler observed, those outside the West cannot resist the temptation of those terrible fruits of progress. The cultures of the world vanish and erode day by day, replaced by a soulless parody of Western culture. [*ETIS* 378]

11. **Humanity fell into modern history like an animal into a trap.**

Looking back on the last several centuries, it is impossible to believe that humanity could have acted differently. The bait was so tempting that the hook went undetected. During the early days of the Enlightenment, Burckhardt notes how "a general victorious and reassuring feeling predominates, one which is fed by the great travels, nature descriptions, and discoveries in the natural sciences" (242). Once a materialistic vision of the world came to dominate, once the nature of mankind was assumed to be primarily an irreligious one, there was no going back. Once man was able to believe that he had the power to make himself into a god, he could not possibly resist. All of his ancient dreams of omnipotence were unleashed as soon as they appeared to finally be within reach. Forgetting the cautionary element in the stories of the Tower of Babel and Prometheus, he threw himself unheeding into the jaws of doom. [*ETIS* 262]

12. **This century is proving to be an interesting spectacle: not for what it does, but for what it undoes.**

Undoubtedly, there are benefits to living through periods of precipitous decline. The darkest fears of the previous century have been realized. What once seemed to be a threatening possibility on the horizon is now the universal landscape. Once our fears have emerged from the shadows into the full brilliance of day, we can see them clearly and they lose something of their menace. Those who warned of doom have been validated and those who celebrated victory have been humbled. The fantasy of political liberation and democracy, the Promethean promises of technology—all are now laid bare in their moments of unraveling. These narratives are falling to pieces and it is plain to see them for the lies they always were. Nothing new is being built, but many old derelict structures are collapsing. The modern project has failed, mankind will not be the new god, and we are lucky enough to witness it. For this gift, may we be truly grateful. [*ETIS* 144]

13. **The bourgeoisie, in the feudal framework, is confined to small urban centers where it is well ordered and disciplined. With the shattering of this framework, the bourgeoisie is unleashed upon society at large and invents the nationalist state, rationalist technology, the multitudinous and anonymous city, industrial society, overpopulation, and finally, the alternating despotism of the mob and the expert.**

In essence, the modern world is the result of the triumph of the bourgeoisie. It is a world where both the values of the peasantry and the aristocracy are vanquished and vanished. By now, the only set of values that carries any weight in the world is that of the bourgeoisie. This is true for both the wealthiest and most powerful, as well as the poorest and most wretched. The concepts and structures that once applied only to a particular class, under particular historical conditions, now freely circulate globally, replacing alternate forms of life and meaning wherever they are found, and reducing the diversity of life and thought to uniformity. And perhaps needless to say, this global system is just as equally prepared to impose itself with fire and the sword as were the colonialists of ages past. The fact that this new form of empire is subtler hardly makes it less brutal. If the feudal system kept individuals and classes fixed within a rigid hierarchy, it also prevented any one particular class from gaining the upper hand. The peasantry, aristocracy, and monarchy were in a constant state of struggle with each other and provided checks and counters to the accumulation of too much power within any one portion of society. It is a fallacy to assume either that the feudal serf was powerless or that the feudal lord was omnipotent. The complex and bloody negotiations between classes under feudalism ensured that balance was maintained in society. This balance, no matter how tenuous it was, no longer exists at all in the modern age. Both the beneficiaries of bourgeois society and its victims are slaves to its logic and consistently uphold its values. [*ETIS* 355]

14. **Where is the world headed? Toward the same transience from**

whence it came.

The pre-Socratics, the mystics of all faiths, and the modern physicists agree, in essence, that the nature of the cosmos is flux and change, circumscribed by an order that maintains balance. There is only one group that denies this evident fact: modern progressive humanity. Forms emerge, they dissolve, and then reform. Like Heraclitus's river, all things are in a constant state of passing away. Claudel writes:

> Each being, as it is Eternity's work,
> so is it Eternity's expression.
> Eternity is present always, and all present things
> pass only into Eternity. (46)

Modern man cannot bear the idea that as he has come into the world, so too will he pass out of it, along with the sum total of his works. And there are no lengths to which he will not go in his attempt to deny this transience. [*ETIS* 221]

15. **A noble society disciplines itself without having to wait for catastrophes to force it to be more disciplined.**

There is no imbalance, either within an individual or a society, that will not be corrected or restored. Imbalance will always resolve itself, one way or another. Climate change, for example, will assuredly correct the imbalances of industrial society by wiping out humanity altogether, if necessary. This is what it means to have a cyclical or traditional view. Imbalance occurs, balance is restored, and so on and so on. The one condition necessitates the emergence of the other, which in turn necessitates resolution. The universe does not leave loose ends. All is woven together in the web of fate. When we perceive imbalance, we can act correctively—or we can stubbornly persist along a disordered path. The latter choice does not mean that balance will not be restored, but it does mean that we will have no choice in the manner by which this restoration will occur. We can correct ourselves or we can wait to be corrected. These are the only options, and it seems clear which choice is likely to be kinder and gentler. [*ETIS* 382]

16. **The surest means of achieving victory are more disastrous than any defeat.**

It is hard not to think of this observation by Gómez Dávila in the context of nuclear weapons. There may be no better illustration of the consequences of valuing victory above all else. The modern mentality rejects the idea that some things are more important than winning. If winning is the only thing that matters, and under those circumstances alone, vaporizing an entire city of men, women, and children can be seen as a reasonable course of action. [*ETIS* 292]

17. **In the last century one might fear that modern ideas would be validated.**
Now it is clear that they were merely victorious.

The greatest minds of the nineteenth and early twentieth century were so terrified that the scientists and industrialists and capitalists would turn out to have been *right* that they failed to notice that their enemies didn't need to be right and didn't care. They only wanted to win, and they did. But their victory does not confirm the truth of their position, it only shows that they have the power to force it upon the world. We do not have to agree with the victors—in fact, the nature of their victory proves the bankruptcy of their ideas. It's easy to win; it's hard to be right. [*ETIS* 260]

18. **We should resign ourselves to the fact that nothing lasts, but refuse to accelerate its passing away.**

To hasten the demise of something old and decayed is not altogether a different impulse from the urge to bring about something progressive and new. In both cases, we can perceive the Promethean compulsion to interfere with the order of the gods, which states: *I will judge how things ought to be and act on that judgment.* This lies at the very heart of the blasphemy of modernity and the deification of mankind. If some moribund form remains, it will pass out of the world according to its own time, according to the mysterious divine hand that turns the wheel of fortune. It is not for us to interfere. Like Prometheus, we will all suffer collectively for our attempts to change the fate of the world. [*ETIS* 173]

19. **Those who predict anything more than indefinite cycles of decline and ascendancy are concealing some dubious product that they want to sell for cash.**

History, religion, and art, the three subjects that may most fruitfully lay claim to wisdom, all teach the same fundamental truth: everything which occurs has occurred before. There is nothing new, only new conditions for the enactment of the same values. Wisdom is gained, accumulated, then lost—and, potentially, recovered. The wheel of fortune is the only metaphor that can offer us an understanding of the world we inhabit. No surprise then to see how little credence is given to it in the modern age. If a truth so obvious and self-evident is denied, we are bound to be wary of the motivations of those who deny it. As Nietzsche observed, it requires a hardy constitution to bear the truth of the nature of fate. The overwhelming majority will prefer any vision of the cosmos that offers them a way out. Progress is simply an idea put forward by those who seek to profit from it. And they too are bound upon the wheel, destined to rise and fall by the will of God. [*ETIS* 171]

20. **Without the spread of oriental cults and the Germanic invasions, the Americanization of the world would have been initiated by Hellenistic civilization, beginning with Rome.**

The fact that the modern world developed as it did, sometime around the sixteenth century, is entirely due to circumstance. Had circumstances been otherwise, we might have seen it emerge centuries, if not millennia, earlier. Certainly we see an abundance of qualities we associate with the modern world present in the Roman empire: a culture degenerating in the realms of art, philosophy, and religion, an ever-expanding hegemonic power, and an imposed uniformity of life and thought. Rome was saved from becoming merely an earlier version of the modern world by two sudden and irresistible explosions. The shocking emergence and growth of Christianity and the devastating incursions of the Germanic tribes provided a much-needed infusion of dynamism, of vital energy, into the sclerotic Roman culture. Of course, Rome ultimately could not withstand this sudden surge of vitality and the Rome of Marcus Aurelius vanished, having been transformed by these new forces. Cultures cannot change internally but only in response to outside powers. This accounts for the hopelessness of the contemporary modern world. There will be no barbarian invasions. There is no force that can challenge it. There is nothing external to it. And so, unlike the Europeans of the fifth century, our modern world will irrevocably descend into death. [*ETIS* 376]

21. **Modern man no longer dares to preach that the individual is born as a blank slate.**
Too many tragedies have taught him that we are the overburdened heirs of our family, our race, our blood.
Blood is not an innocent liquid, but the viscous paste of history.

How much of the drama of our lives and global current events has been scripted for us! Like a phantom limb, the past continues to act upon us and direct our course, whether we like it or not. Rupert Sheldrake and the emerging field of epigenetics confirm that the weight of history is carried within our blood. The traumas of our ancestors are alive in us. The notion that each generation is responsible for expiating the crimes of the previous ones is quite universal in traditional societies. The modern is the one who mistakenly assumes that what has passed before him has no bearing on his life in the present. "What has it all got to do with me?" he cries. His ignorance will not save him from the consequences of what he carries. Needless to say, the implications of this fact are much darker and more pessimistic than the contemporary anti-racist or his conservative opponent realizes. [*ETIS* 176]

22. **History is a succession of nights and days—brief days and long nights.**

"O tasteless and ignorant age!" shrieked Catullus. Those moments in history when humanity has lived with wisdom, in concert with nature and the eternal laws of the cosmos, have been necessarily brief. Mankind has more often chosen to ignore timeless truths and descend into disorder. The sacred nature of the world—being timeless and impervious to human thought and action—is always there for us to rediscover, but in the absence of the notion of God, which is the only context that provides ideas with intelligibility and meaning, it cannot be recaptured. We have seen, throughout history, moments when humanity has acted in denial of this greater context, which then usher in generations of ignorance and chaos. A new day will dawn, but who can say how quickly the light of the sun will be darkened by storm clouds? [*ETIS* 261]

23. **The true crime of colonialism was to reduce the great Asiatic civilizations to mere suburbs of the West.**

Montaigne writes: "I very much fear that we shall have greatly hastened the decline and ruin of this other hemisphere by our contact" (277). As horrific as the human cost of colonialism undeniably was, over centuries of genocide and exploitation, the loss of the magnificent, vast, and infinitely complex cultures of Central and South America, Africa, and then Asia was more tragic still. As Gandhi knew, India could withstand the brutality of the British, but would perish if it adopted their ways and culture. The irreplaceable loss of the myriad diversity of the cultures of the world brought with it the imposition of a uniform order, which has, in the twentieth and twenty-first centuries, produced a single global culture—the culture of the modern world. The blame for this surely lies upon the European imperialists who exported industrialism, capitalism, and democracy with the gun and the lash. The varied richness of the world's great civilizations has been buried beneath a paltry simulacrum of Western culture. As Gómez Dávila well understood as a South American intellectual, the tragic destiny of the former colonies was simply to imitate, in the most vulgar fashion, the culture of the colonizer. The terms which the former colonies were left with to understand their place were inevitably dictated by the modern West, and if the nations of Europe were cast aside as imperial overlords, the Western mentality continued to work its baleful influence. The history of the modern world is the history of the triumph of the blandest, most degenerate unipolarity. A uniform world allows no space for diversity and plurality. All must be as one. [*ETIS* 153]

24. **Luckily, the world cannot be explained. (What would the world be if it could be explained to humanity?)**

As Montaigne observed, even if everything that has been known by humanity in its entirety could be reproduced reliably within one man, it would pale in comparison to that which is unknown and can never be known. The means of observation of even the most curious and diligent mind are paltry, wretched, and insurmountably restricted. The modern world, infatuated with mankind's supposed ability to wield omnipotent power by means of reason, cannot abide this notion and denies it outright. So, while modern man is content to assume that the vision of the world conjured by his pitiless rationality effectively circumscribes the whole of existence, we can take comfort in the knowledge that he is assuredly wrong. How could we bear it if we thought that the richness and mysteries of life could be understood by minds as timorous and callow as our own? Of course, modern man cannot be said to truly bear it either. He will cling to his vanity even as his mind, body, and soul collapse beneath its weight. [*ETIS* 193]

25. **Fools believe that contemporary humanity is unique in knowing certain important things, but there is nothing important that humanity has not known since the beginning.**

One of the chief justifications made of the modern world is its claim to knowledge. Modern man believes that he knows things that previous eras could not possibly understand. We might ask in passing, what such knowledge has done to benefit humanity, but leaving aside this line of inquiry for the moment, it is even more clear that none of the vital insights that modern man has achieved are in any way unique. The idea that one particular age of mankind has privileged access to what, in the final analysis, must be accurately termed *timeless* wisdom, is a very old one. Lucretius wrote: "Indeed, the universe, as I believe, is new. The world is quite fresh, and came into being not long ago. So some arts are still being perfected, and are even now advancing, and many things are now being discovered about the art of navigation" (cited in Montaigne, 276). Things only appear unique in the eyes of the observer, the ever-watchful eye of the cosmos has seen it all so many times before. Montaigne puts it thus: "We do not move forwards, but rather wander, turning this way and that. We return over our tracks" (275). Mankind's knowledge is only ever waxing or waning. [*ETIS* 196]

26. **Man's knowledge of himself increases until the seventeenth century, then declines gradually. In this century it finally bottoms out.**

The progressive insists on the value of the increase in man's technical knowledge, but he is conspicuously silent when it comes to the matter of man's self-knowledge. Certainly this is because even the most delusional progressive cannot claim that modern man understands himself. In fact, for most, it has been assumed that there is no point in trying to understand ourselves. Even the heroic task of confronting the monsters of the subconscious has been replaced by the most recent trend in psychology: behavioral therapy. Let us not bother trying to understand our motivations, fears, and desires. That requires too much uncertainty; it takes a lifetime to achieve, and depends upon the patient's willingness to be truthful and courageous. Modern man says: "Never mind. Instead of trying to understand myself, I'll just focus on my behaviors. They, at any rate, are less mysterious and confusing." Thus, if the patient cannot reckon with himself like a man, he will try to program himself like a robot. How many in this century have had the courage, like Montaigne, to sit down and explore his various ideas and sentiments? To plumb the depths of the self? Who among us moderns could possibly say, as Montaigne did: "I study myself more than any other subject. This is my metaphysics, this is my physics" (353). It is the outward-facing world that concerns modern man: a world forever limited by the perceptual apparatus. The limitless internal world, however, as it resists the quantifiable logic of data, is ignored. As the Irish mystic philosopher John Moriarty reminds us, we have learned to walk on the moon without having learned what it properly means to walk upon the earth. The twentieth and twenty-first centuries have produced an extraordinary amount of information, most of it relating to the nonhuman world, but produced little to no insights about human nature. If in ancient times, according to Aristarchus, there were seven wise men in the entire world, it seems likely that our world contains not a single one. [*ETIS* 397]

27. The forces that will destroy a civilization collaborate from its birth with the forces that construct it.

Just as universal suffrage was the goal of modern democratic society, we can see now that it will also be the means of its destruction. When the voice of the people is sovereign, it guarantees the absolutism of the state. As Burckhardt observed:

> The concept of equality is a two-edged one here. It turns into the abdication of the individual, because the more universal any possession is, the fewer individual defenders it finds. Once people have become accustomed to the state as the sole guardian of rights and public welfare, even the *will* to decentralization no longer helps. . . . In general, despite all the talk about freedom, peoples and governments demand unlimited state power internally. (219)

Suffrage, which aims at empowering the individual, eliminates any protection he might have otherwise hoped for against the cruelty and intolerance of his fellows. Democracy opens the door for demagogic tyrants to step through. [*ETIS* 348]

28. Every event assumes its form as the result of all the forces at work at the place and time of its creation. All things descend indirectly from the totality.

The ultimate illegibility of history is due to the fact that we are unable to properly understand the totality. The traditional view of history, the providentialist view, simply states that history as a whole is the exclusive domain of the divine, which, by definition, explains very little. All facts and particulars are irreducible, unique, and self-sufficient because they have been arranged according to the divine hand. The modern, progressive view suggests that past and present can only be understood in relation to an ideal future state, toward which it unerringly moves. Thus, historical circumstances are reduced to a logical sequence of events, with no particular significance or value whatsoever. This, of course, is the position of Marx and Hegel. The third attempt to read history is the reductionist, which argues that one set of particular facts or circumstances can be used to explain every other. This final method successfully conveys the interconnected nature of historical facts but only does so by radically and arbitrarily narrowing its focus. Why should one set of facts determine all others more than any other set of facts? In other words, there is no one schema—nor a clever combination of them—that can account for the complexity of historical processes. The task of the student of history is a noble if not a happy one. This is why history, for Gómez Dávila, was subservient to metaphysics. History cannot be successfully understood by man without faith in God. [*ETIS* 357]

29. The "wheel of fortune" is a better analogy for history than the "evolution of humanity."

Darwin's assumption of natural struggle leading to more and more successful forms has been used as an implicit justification for greater horrors than modern man tends to realize. Believing that the will to change is synonymous with progress has certainly led, as Burckhardt observed, to the "eradication of the inferior races of mankind, of the savages as remnants of arrested developmental stages" (236).

If man's struggles do *not* lead him inevitably forward, which now is difficult to deny, we must accept that there is no particular meaning or direction in history. We ceaselessly turn upon the wheel; the goal is not to break free from it or to rise above it, but only to understand the principles that set it into motion and by whose will it continues to revolve. [*ETIS* 283]

30. The world is a failed quest that the noble soul strives to complete.

In the Arthurian legend of the Fisher King, the land suffers and wastes away as a consequence of the king's wound, which will not heal. This wound, of course, is impotence: the loss of generative power and fertility. Only the most-pure knight can heal this devastating injury to both mankind and the land by means of the Holy Grail, the Holy Blood. We may certainly understand this story in terms of the cyclical battles of Summer and Winter, growth and decay. What manner of restoration can the authentic reactionary really hope for? Only one that comes with the beginning of a new cycle. [*ETIS* 102]

31. Peace only thrives in dying nations, under the iron fist of tyranny.

The dream of peace is not one that comes to mankind in the vigorous spring and summertime ages of nations. It is a drowsy vision, heavy with sleep and close to death. The *pax romana* could only have come to fruition both during a period in which the vitality of Rome was in decline and under its most brutally repressive form of governance. Ultimately, peace can only be gained through a totalizing eradication of difference. It is a product of the most repressive uniformity, relying on the apparatus of an all-powerful state. Great wars are increasingly a thing of the past. It is almost impossible to imagine the massive conflagrations of the twentieth century in our own twilight age. For all that peace reigns, however, there is not less suffering in the world but more. What modern man has failed to recognize is that peace does not represent the end of suffering. In ages of peace, mankind only turns his violence and viciousness against himself. [*ETIS* 89]

II
God and the Gods

1. **For the intelligent man, faith is the only remedy for anguish. The fool can be cured by "reason," "progress," alcohol, and work.**

The imbecile of the modern world has countless means of distracting himself from his sorrows and fears. He can convince himself that things will get better, and that people are essentially reasonable. Generally speaking, the fool assumes that it will work out somehow. If not, he can always bury himself in the quotidian minutiae of his life or dull his mind with drugs and alcohol. In either case, he allows himself to forget and live some semblance of a happy life. The thinking person, however, is unable to comfort himself. He perceives that he has no reason whatsoever to believe that things will get better, nor can he have any confidence in humanity's ability to correct its course. The intelligent man cannot be distracted, no matter how hard he tries. As man is fundamentally undeserving of our confidence, we can only place our confidence in the hands of God. [*ETIS* 451]

2. **The Church's function is not to adapt Christianity to the world, nor even to adapt the world to Christianity; her function is to maintain a counterworld within the world.**

We must remember that Gómez Dávila's glosses are commentaries on other texts, conversations with his favorite authors, and, frequently, arguments. Here we may perceive a response to Chesterton, who writes:

> Progress should mean that we are always changing the world to suit the vision. Progress does mean (just now) that we are always changing the vision . . . Progress should mean that we are always walking towards the New Jerusalem. It does mean that the New Jerusalem is always walking away from us. (113)

It is clear enough that we have utterly abandoned the path toward the New Jerusalem and that our vision has failed us. But Gómez Dávila takes Chesterton's remarks a step further: the world itself, regardless of the extent to which we attempt to shape it in accord with our vision, is incompatible with the kingdom of God. The task of the Church cannot be to make this world something that it is not. The greatest achievement of the Church is to gesture toward and make a space where we might encounter another world. We cannot change the world we inhabit, nor can we ever hope to dwell entirely in another, but we may catch a fleeting glimpse of a vast mysterious country filled with unfathomable wonders. And, perhaps, like the ancient heroes of the Irish fairytales, we might hope to abide there awhile and taste its exquisite fruits. [*ETIS* 455]

3. **Because he presumptuously behaved as though he was capable of giving fullness to the world, modern man sees it become more hollow each day.**

Modern man hates the beauty of the world because it reminds him that, as he could not create that beauty, his domination of the world is forever incomplete. He hates God for the same reason. If man, the creator and source of all value, could not create something, then it must have no value. Far from the petulance of the modern mentality, the revenant soul gazes into the water and dissolves in the sublimity of a force that is far beyond itself. We can hear the cries of Claudel:

> My God,
> I see and judge myself, and I no longer count myself
> for anything.
> You gave me life: I give it back. I prefer you
> take back all.
> I see myself at last and I am desolation, and the sorrow
> within opens my liquid eye upon all. (52)

Modern man has triumphed over God, which in turn has given him no reason to live. As Karl Jaspers puts it in *Man in the Modern Age*: "'There is no God,' cry the masses more and more vociferously; and with the loss of his God man loses his sense of values—is, as it were, massacred because he feels himself of no account" (157). If God is dead, the death of humanity can be considered collateral damage. [*ETIS* 285]

4. **Faith is not knowledge of the object.**
But rather communication with it.

What theologians have failed to understand, according to Gómez Dávila, is that the nature of divinity lies beyond the scope of human reason. In this we can perceive his debt to Kierkegaard. An intelligible god would be no god at all, but nothing more than a human construction, unworthy of love or worship. We can only worship something that is profoundly beyond or outside of ourselves. This does not mean, however, that humanity can ever be utterly disconnected from the divine source of life. If we cannot know God, we can at least speak to God, and open ourselves to the possibility of Him speaking back to us. [*ETIS* 196]

5. **Religious thought does not advance, like scientific thought, but rather deepens.**

The great European scientific innovations and discoveries of the fifteenth and sixteenth centuries were immediately put to use in conquering and subjugating the world. In our own time, we see scientific thought culminate in fantasies of space travel and colonizing other planets. This is no coincidence; the scientific mindset is, in essence, a colonizing one. All that exists must be brought within its purview and understanding. Science is a pitiless conquistador. Religious thought progresses on the opposite axis. It turns its descending gaze upon forgotten graves and tombs. It finds "the world in a grain of sand." If science seeks to dissolve the universe in the crucible of human thought, religion seeks to dissolve human thought within the harmony of the universe. [*ETIS* 409]

6. **As we cannot find shelter in the Gospel alone, we likewise cannot take refuge in the seed of the oak tree but only beside its crooked trunk, beneath its disordered branches.**

Here we see Gómez Dávila, the realist, acknowledging that for all the weaknesses of the modern Church, it remains the best and last hope for us in this time of darkness. While Gómez Dávila does not appear to have been familiar with the works of the French Traditionalist René Guénon, he seems here to arrive at a similar conclusion: that spirituality depends on the existence of real, living institutions and traditions, no matter how flawed. The contemporary Church has lost its way, but it is still the repository of two thousand years' worth of Christian history and tradition. [*ETIS* 245]

7. **When it is not Christ himself who preaches, the preacher of the**

kingdom of God ends up preaching the kingdom of man.

While Gómez Dávila dutifully attended mass, he had no interest in sermons and in fact suggested that they should be ignored. This reminds us of an observation by Kierkegaard—a great influence on Gómez Dávila's religious thought—that there was only ever one real Christian. While something of the nature of God can be revealed to the believer through the rites and liturgies of the Church, there is almost nothing to be learned about God that comes from the mouth of man. Invariably, and we see this now almost universally in the Catholic Church: when man speaks, he speaks of man, not God. [*ETIS* 177]

8. **Love of humanity is often used as an excuse to forget God with a clear conscience.**

The modern project, in essence, is nothing other than the deification of man. Clearly, the elimination of God is a vital necessity for the success of this project. The priests of progress almost always justify their beliefs by saying that they are for the good of humanity. The socialist and even the vulgar capitalist claim to act out of love for the species. Mankind will be free and prosperous, and therefore happy, they argue. But both secretly dream of the day when man will supplant God. One sees this perhaps most often among the so-called Christian socialists, forwhom the Kingdom of God is replaced by an earthly paradise where all will be as one. If they truly loved man, they would understand that it is only in God that man can find peace and joy. A godless world can only be one of dejection and misery. [*ETIS* 127]

9. **More than a Christian, perhaps I'm a pagan who believes in Christ.**

To paraphrase Chesterton, the pagan is happy about everything but miserable about everything else, while the Christian is miserable about everything but happy about everything else. Is life filled with joy, meaning, and an immanent divinity, while the gods above are largely indifferent to us, or is life a tedious and never-ending battle against sin and wickedness, wretched due to the insurmountable gulf between being and God, but redeemed after death in the joyful reunion with our Creator? For Mircea Eliade, Christianity completes and redeems paganism by providing an overarching destiny, one which moves us ever onward toward salvation. Christianity, for Eliade, offers the pagan wheel of birth, death, and rebirth an escape. The endless bloody rites of the pagan are softened by the image of a God of love and forgiveness. It is not coincidental that the notion of God who loves his wretched creations should shock us. It is a truly radical idea. If the gods have fated man to struggle, the pagan accepts this, without the expectation either of eternal reward or eternal torment. What might the idea of a pagan who believes in Christ suggest? Chesterton writes: "We are all revenants; all living Christians are dead pagans walking about" (162). Perhaps it is somehow akin to the attempts by Carl Jung, W. B. Yeats, and others who sought to reconcile the pagan and the Christian visions of the cosmos. From the perspective of Neoplatonism, we may suppose that Gómez Dávila indicates an interest in the notion that all things both natural and cosmological emanate from a single unitary creative source, the various pagan gods understood to be particular forms deriving therefrom. Perhaps it is simply gesturing toward the idea of immanence, that the light of the divine can still be perceived within the corporeal world, that the sacred can be detected in the caress of a thigh or in the rustling of the leaves in the trees. [*ETIS* 113]

10. The death of God is an interesting opinion, but it is not one that affects God.

Modern man takes his ideas so seriously because he does not fundamentally believe that the objective world actually exists. We think that our ideas about things are more important than the things themselves, or rather we end up thinking that the things themselves have no reality, but only our ideas about them. Taken in this context, man's thoughts and observations about the nature or the existence of God are really quite comical. The Daoist sage Zhuangzi tells the story of a conversation between a turtle and a frog who lives at the bottom of a well. The frog believes that there is no body of water bigger or more beautiful than his well. When the turtle informs him that there are vast rivers and lakes and oceans, the frog angrily insists that he is lying. Modern man only believes that his ideas matter because he thinks his mind is all there is. [*ETIS* 134]

11. **Humanity is the only god that is totally false.**

Gómez Dávila is surprisingly sympathetic to the pagan gods. Krishna, Odin, Quetzalcoatl, Pan, and the Dagda are all true and real—though perhaps, for Gómez Dávila, slightly less true and less real than Christ. All religions maintain and preserve the sacred conception of man and the cosmos. The only meaningful exception is the religion that claims to be no religion at all, which is the religion of humanism. Certainly, any kind of religious sentiment is superior to even the most clearheaded and rational atheism. While the atheists and the humanists reject the idea of God, they nevertheless put an idol in its place and that idol is man. As long as the pagan religions affirm the timeless traditional truths, they have a claim to authenticity and validity, even for Gómez Dávila. [*ETIS* 294]

12. **That which concerns the Christ of the Gospels is not the economic situation of the poor, but the moral condition of the rich.**

The contemporary humanist or socialist Christians make the colossal mistake of assuming that the call for transformation found in the Gospels applies not just to the spiritual and inner conditions of man, but to his economic conditions as well. The poor of the Gospels are blessed because they are poor and the rich are damned because they are rich. To interpret this as a call for the improvement of the material conditions of the poor is insanity. [*ETIS* 455]

13. **The basic problem of every former colony—the problem of intellectual slavishness, of impoverished tradition, of second-rate spirituality, of inauthentic civilization, of inevitable and shameful imitation—has been resolved for me with the utmost simplicity: Catholicism is my native land.**

Gómez Dávila's status as a Latin American intellectual was a challenging one and occupied much of his thought. While he appeared to resent his Colombian heritage, he certainly had the means to settle elsewhere and nevertheless chose to remain in Colombia for his entire adult life. The fact that his ideas were not appreciated in his homeland matters little, as they most certainly would have received the same frosty reception in any modern society, and he was obviously aware of this fact. Therefore it is in Catholicism, so deeply entrenched in the Latin American world, that Gómez Dávila finds his identity. That he was Colombian is thus merely circumstantial in his view. [*ETIS* 72]

14. **It is not primitive cults that discredit religion, but rather North American sects.**

Toward the end of his life, the German writer Ernst Jünger observed that "sects are taking off. This is a sign that the churches are no longer really playing their part" (118). A moribund Catholicism facilitates the growth and popularity of groups like the Mormons, Jehovah's

Witnesses, Seventh Day Adventists, Scientologists, and Christian Scientists. Surrounded by the likes of these, even the most frightening and strange pagan mysteries can be seen for what they really are: expressions of true religion. [*ETIS* 470]

15. **So great is the distance between God and human intelligence that only an infantile theology is not childish.**

The more complex our ideas become, the more our foolishness is revealed. The most sophisticated and elaborate product of the human intellect is nothing more than a monument to itself, to its own grandeur. Such ideas have no substance. At least in the simplicity of the child there is clarity and honesty. Modern man takes ideas seriously in inverse proportion to their worth. The scholarly debates of theologians are inscrutable, but any child who possesses even a passing familiarity with fairy tales can understand the act of receiving communion. If Christianity is an infantile theology, then that is precisely where its power lies. [*ETIS* 171]

16. **Modern man imagines that in order to cure the soul's infection, it is enough to merely open the windows rather than to actually take out the trash.**

The remedies that are generally offered to modern man for his soul's sickness are the equivalent of trying to make a dying patient comfortable or to distract him from the fact that he is dying. The patient does not imagine that he could recover, and modern society does not pretend to be able to heal him. If we continue to try to address symptoms rather than causes, we know what will happen. If something stinks, modern man would rather get an air freshener to disguise the smell, than clean what is dirty or throw it away. [*ETIS* 336]

17. **The believer is not a possessor of hereditary land titles, but rather a sea captain upon the shores of an unexplored continent.**

Faith does not entitle us to rewards; it opens a vast uncertain horizon before us. It is not a secure and stable inheritance, but an ongoing adventure, fraught with peril and requiring our utmost courage. As Chesterton writes:

> [T]o a Christian existence is a story, which may end up in any way. In a thrilling novel (that purely Christian product) the hero is not eaten by cannibals but it is essential to the existence of the thrill that he might be eaten by cannibals. The hero must (so to speak) be an eatable hero. (148)

Faith is not a state of placid, self-assured retirement, but a heroic condition, dangerous, where every moment is filled with life-or-death decisions. [*ETIS* 70]

18. **Resignation ought not to be an exercise in stoicism, but a surrendering of oneself into the hands of the divine.**

Throughout Gómez Dávila's religious writings we can perceive the influence of the revelatory poetry of Claudel:

> Oh, my God, my being sighs to yours.
> Deliver me from myself, deliver this being from contingency.
> I am free, but deliver me from freedom. (43)

Like the other members of the Catholic Revival movement, Claudel's is an anti-intellectual, anti-rational faith, which resists any attempt at systematic scholarly understanding. Following Claudel, Gómez Dávila's experience of the divine is arrived at through the realm of aesthetics and revelation. Indeed, how can the sacred be expected to be understood by a mechanism that is so foreign to it? The cool and calm self-sufficiency of Marcus Aurelius is superseded here by the joyful and ecstatic throwing of oneself at the feet of the divine. For Gómez Dávila, union with God cannot be achieved through the self, but rather by an abandonment and stripping bare of the self. [*ETIS* 353]

19. **An irreligious society cannot endure the truth of the human condition. It prefers a fictional narrative, even if it's a stupid one.**

In the absence of religion, the modern Western world has come no closer to the utopia imagined by the *philosophes* of the Enlightenment. Secularism was meant to liberate mankind from the childish superstitious terrors of the Church and, in so doing, allow the free spirit of man to ascend unfettered toward greater and greater heights. In the end it merely exchanged an imperfect master for a disastrous one. Gómez Dávila's concern for society ultimately remains that of defending the cause of freedom. For him it is simply that the most dangerous form of tyranny is the tyranny of the masses, facilitated by the democratic, rationalistic energies brought into the world through the revolutions of the eighteenth and nineteenth centuries. [*ETIS* 200]

20. **Ritual is the discreet guardian of spirituality.**

Through the symbols that resonate deep within the subconscious, which give life to what we term "tradition," ritual and liturgy preserves the nature of spirituality. For Gómez Dávila, this is the reason pagan forms of worship can be seen as authentic. The ancient pagan religions were nothing if not primarily and fundamentally ritualistic. The pagan mysteries and initiatic cults thus have an even greater claim to religiosity than the modern Catholic church, purged of its liturgies. In the absence of ritual, religion is increasingly reduced to a set of ethical considerations, which lead mankind not to a deeper connection with the divine, but to a greater investment in human society. When ritual perishes, spirituality itself is soon to follow. [*ETIS* 410]

21. **The soul is degraded when the body is lazy.**

That the modern world both produces physical weakness and infirmity, while it denies the existence of the soul, is not coincidental. The two factors work in concert. By privileging the comforts of the body, modern society ensures that the soul will die. Both body and soul require vigor and vitality. In a body that is inert, how can the soul rise to communion with the divine? If the body lies in torpor, it becomes a swamp that drags the soul down with it. The body must strive, just as the soul does. [*ETIS* 252]

22. **The shadow of God is cast between man and nothingness.**

The radical nature of Christianity lies in its positing of a benevolent God, which actively *loves* humanity. When considered in its proper context, this is a truly shocking proposition and in some degree accounts for the incredible global success of the Christian religion. The amazing novelty of the figure of Christ, which appears in the gospels, indicates a tectonic shift in religious understanding. The indifference of the pagan gods, constrained as they are within the same threads of fate that determine human lives, as well as the abstract and impersonal sense of a pervasive world soul or source, which is found among the Neoplatonists, do not necessarily offer man a path out of his existential crises. Of course, we may debate whether or not such a path is needful, but for Gómez Dávila, the simple and non-intellectual premise of God's love for humanity was the driving force behind his Christian faith. For all his wide-ranging scholarly accomplishments,

Gómez Dávila had no interest whatsoever in the debates of Christian theologians. The attempt to understand the nature of God and his grace in intellectual, logical terms was, for him, irreverent. For Gómez Dávila, the most important task of the Church is to preserve the mystery of God through ritual. [*ETIS* 318]

23. **Modern history is the dialogue between two men: one who believes in God, the other who believes he is god.**

The revolutionary struggles of the eighteenth and nineteenth century were about more than democracy and political liberation. In their deepest natures, these struggles were cosmic ones. The project of the Enlightenment, of which the revolutions were merely the outward, political manifestation, primarily targeted religion and the sacred conception of the world. The counter-revolutions, in turn, fought to restore the old order, which, again, was a fundamentally religious one. The explosive impact of the Protestant Reformation and the wars and upheavals that resulted from it, of course, repeat this same pattern in the previous generation. Thus, we can see modern history as an ongoing struggle for the right to define the terms of humanity and the cosmos. One on side we have the sacred, religious vision of the world, emanating from God. On the other side we have the rationalistic, interpretative vision, deriving from human reason. Certainly, the consequence of the secular project has not been to eradicate the idea of God, but only to place man in His role. In the twenty-first century, it is difficult to say that this struggle—or dialogue, as Gómez Dávila sees it—has not been decisively concluded. If it was once a dialogue, it is now a monologue. Like Satan in Milton's *Paradise Lost*, contemporary man is nothing if not a solipsist. [*ETIS* 236]

24. **We do not not accuse modern man of having killed God, since**

that crime is not within his power, but rather of having killed *the gods*.
God remains untroubled, but the universe withers and decays because specific deities have passed away.

Mankind may not be able to harm the Creator, but he can certainly brutalize and disfigure that which has been created. The source of divinity is immune to man's evil, but the manifestations of divinity are not. Presented with a sacred world, inhabited by sacred beings, modern man has done everything he can to drive that sacredness out of the world and has largely succeeded. God remains, as always, but the fauns and dryads and their like have been annihilated by modernity. We are now seeing what a world looks like when all the emanations of the divine have been destroyed. We don't need to worry about God—the loss of the enchanted world is quite enough of a tragedy. [*ETIS* 159]

25. **The impertinent attempt to justify "the ways of God to man" transforms God into an irritable schoolteacher who devises lessons, which are simultaneously cruel and childish.**

The criticisms of religion one is so accustomed to hearing in today's world are, without exception, the result of the attempt to make the divine will comprehensible to human reason. As soon as the nature of divinity is reduced to terms that can be accommodated and digested by the human mind, it can only appear—as it does to so many irreligious people—arbitrary, infantile, and vicious. The contemporary Church, in other words, has sacrificed the meaning of God in order to make Him intelligible. Once religion is expected to enter into dialogue with the world, it loses its purpose. The point, which Gómez Dávila returns to time and again, is that the ways of God cannot be understood by man. The power of the divine lies entirely in its mystery and separation from the world of men. [*ETIS* 389]

26. The gods are like peasants who will accompany man only as far as the gates of great cities.

It is not coincidental that one interpretation of the word "pagan" refers to the rural. Nor that one finds throughout the Old Testament an association of the urban world with sin, wickedness, and godlessness. With the exception of the Greeks and the Romans, who might have initiated the modern world millennia earlier had it not been for their unique historical conditions, the sacred world is universally situated in the outlandish and remote wilderness. The clearing of the forests—here we may think of Charlemagne cutting down the sacred Germanic groves—serves to prepare the land for urbanization. Just as the peasant recognizes the urban world as alien and inhospitable to his worldview, the gods, as well, have no place in the concrete jungles. This is because the city is the only landscape that is completely dominated by man and his reason. The rural world can accommodate the nonhuman and the divine, and man cannot but perceive his dependence on the greater powers there. The city allows humanity to pretend that he is sovereign and omnipotent. This is the concept at the heart of the profane urban project. [*ETIS* 212]

27. The problems of humanity cannot be defined with any degree of precision and they certainly cannot be solved. One who hopes that Christianity will solve them has ceased to be a Christian.

At best, we may say that humanity's problems are, in essence, cosmological ones. As he is unable to grasp the totality of the workings of the cosmos, man is unable to properly account for the nature of his problems. Furthermore, we might say that the existence of these problems itself is inscribed into the laws of the cosmos. The idea of solving them could only occur to man once he has severed his connection with the universe. The purpose of Christianity or religion in general is not to eliminate or assuage these problems, but to simply put them into context and offer solace. Religion does not show us the way out of our struggles; it gives us the strength to confront them. Solutions, on the other hand, are unquestionably the domain of the Devil. God does not make promises or bargains—the Devil does. When man finds that a problem has been solved for him, he need only look to who profits thereby. [*ETIS* 143]

28. **To quote an author is to show that one is incapable of assimilating him.**

Someone who has truly understood what they have read does not need to employ quotations. True understanding of a text or an author consists in recognizing that wisdom is not a private acquisition, but a universal divine stream that flows through individuals of genius throughout the ages. The goal of reading is to perceive those traces of wisdom that are familiar to us because they were already present in ourselves. Cicero never said anything that should not be obvious to anyone with a brain. His wisdom, the wisdom of any worthy author, is timeless and derived from the divine. Thus, to quote Cicero is really a misattribution. Reading connects us to God. [*ETIS* 123]

29. **Hierarchies are heavenly.**
In hell all are equal.

If Milton's Satan reigns in Hell, he only does so amidst the incoherent clamor of parliamentary democracy. Where Heaven is a well-ordered and peaceful hierarchy, Hell is the discordant chaos of each individual shouting to be heard. We can never be alike in virtue, but we can all be equal in sin. [*ETIS* 245]

30. **It is not the existence of God that democratic atheism disputes, but rather his identity.**

Atheism is really a misnomer. The modern atheist believes in many things with the same degree of religious fervor as those he derides as superstitious fools. In fact, as Gómez Dávila suggests here, it is not even that the atheist doesn't believe in God—he just calls God by a different name, such as "science," or "progress," or "humanity." In order to identify the gods of modern atheistic man, we need only look at what he worships. [*ETIS* 338]

31. **It is not so much that the modern mentality denies the existence of God—it can't even make sense of the word.**

The ultimate spiritual tragedy of the modern world is that believing in God means nothing when the conceptual apparatus for understanding God is lacking. The cosmological viewpoint of modern man is so fundamentally incompatible with the idea of the sacred or the divine that faith itself becomes incoherent. This is why we see the purpose of religion in the modern age becoming increasingly oriented toward moralism and humanism. In a world where the material conditions of humanity are seen as primary, the Church must either allow itself to become obsolete or abandon the project of the spiritual cultivation of man, in favor of entering the discourse around the challenges facing contemporary society. As soon as religion is expected to engage with or offer solutions to contemporary problems, it has lost its role as the preserver and guardian of tradition and timeless truth. In the face of a humanistic and anthropocentric Christianity, paganism looks to become the last true repository of a spirituality unclouded by human and social concerns. [*ETIS* 132]

32. **After experiencing what an age with practically no religion consists of, Christianity is learning to write the history of paganism with respect and sympathy.**

It is striking that in reading Chesterton's *Orthodoxy*, which contains his most fervent defense of Christianity, we find one of the most articulate and sensitive modern analyses of paganism. In the face of the scientific and materialist onslaught, Chesterton was able to perceive that paganism sought to provide a solution to the problem, which, in his view, only Christianity succeeded in solving. While in ages past Christianity and paganism battled for the soul of the West, the modern world has brought forth a new enemy, godlessness, which brings them together. If, as Chesterton puts it, the pagan views nature as a mother and Christianity views her merely as a sister, the modern denies any personhood or agency to nature altogether. If the pagan finds virtue in balance, in the mixture of good and evil within all, and the Christian finds it in the paradoxical triumph of simultaneously praising all that is good and condemning all that is evil, the modern secularists can only, in Chesterton's phrase, "throw darkness and confusion on themselves" (103). [*ETIS* 449]

33. **Christianity completes paganism by adding confidence in God to the fear of the divine.**

Chesterton was not altogether wrong when he argued that the pagan is confronted by an essentially indifferent cosmos. The miracle of Christianity is that it poses a benevolent, caring heart at the core of the universe. Thus, while the pagan can only experience awe and terror, the Christian can also experience comfort. Having said that, Chesterton is a sophisticated enough thinker to acknowledge that the pagan is afforded countless little joys and pleasures that the Christian is incapable of appreciating. The Christian pays for his benevolent cosmos by giving up the laughter in the trees. [*ETIS* 410]

34. **For one who lives in the modern world, it is not just the soul's immortality that is subject to doubt, but its mere existence.**

Dante said: "doubting pleases me no less than knowing" (*Inferno*, XI, 93). In ages past, the nature of the soul was debated and hotly contested. To question or even to doubt the nature of the soul or God is highly amenable to religion. The Jewish rabbinical tradition is built entirely upon this. In the modern world of today, the nature of the soul or God is not questioned at all—it is denied outright or dismissed as irrelevant without a thought. The spiritual questions that so preoccupied and even tortured man have now been settled because he has now rejected the very categories of thought required to understand them. In a world where everything is superficial, the concepts of immortality, soul, and God have no meaning. [*ETIS* 368]

35. **Let us deceive no one: the devil can deliver the material goods he promises.**

Modern society is exclusively oriented around the fulfillment of material needs and desires. For the modern Church, even the Christ of the gospels is reconceived as some sort of proto-communist, whose purpose is reduced to promoting an equitable redistribution of goods. Among the fairy and folktales, however, which in this age may be seen as one of the last true repositories of traditional wisdom, the fate of those who lust after material wealth is unambiguous. Prosperity always comes at a price, but if prosperity is considered to be the highest value, that price will always seem worth paying. Man will find out too late what he has bargained away, and the identity of whom he has bargained with. [*ETIS* 323]

36. **We may beg for mercy. But by what right do we demand justice?**

For Gómez Dávila, the anthropocentric focus on worldly matters, at the expense of metaphysical or spiritual concerns, necessarily degrades mankind. The cry for justice, which has been growing louder and more clamorous since the Age of Revolutions, is emblematic of the modern idea that mankind is able to set the terms of the human condition. The timeless truths, which have come to mankind through revelation rather than through the instrument of his reason, do not include justice. Mercy—or the value of kindness, gentleness, and pity—is certainly one of these truths. But as the natural world knows nothing of justice, neither can man. Neither the laws of the cosmos nor the mind of God or the gods accommodate this idea. Justice is a purely interpretive concept, born from the narrow consciousness of the rational mind. What is justice to one is injustice to another, and on and on. Each man who is asked "What is justice?" can only ever reply based on what seems right to him, given his unique perspective and circumstances. Thus, justice—like all modern ideas—becomes the self-interested justification for any action whatsoever. What horrors have not been committed in the name of justice, as with its kindred concepts of peace and freedom? Montaigne writes:

> [A]s the Stoics hold, nature herself in most of her works goes against justice. That, as the Cyrenaics contend, there is nothing inherently just; customs and laws make justice. That, according to the Theodorians, theft, sacrilege, and all sorts of crimes are lawful for the sage if he knows that they are profitable to him. There is no remedy. (352)

Any idea that comes from man rather than from God will inevitably be corrupted and put to misuse. [*ETIS* 203]

37. **Every rebellion against the order of man is noble, unless it is actually a rebellion against the order of the world in disguise.**

It is an unfortunate fact that resistance to the nature of things is so often disguised as resistance to the injustice of man. The great revolutionaries have always struggled against the divine order, but since they can never hope to win that struggle, they generally claim to be fighting against the false and iniquitous dominion of mankind's social and political structures. Tragically, the true battles against the laws of man would be in favor of the laws of nature and the gods—and thus these positions have been, and will continue to be, dismissed as reactionary. [*ETIS* 101]

38. "To renounce the world" ceases to be an achievement and becomes a temptation as Progress marches onward.

If the world is beautiful and good, renunciation is a valorous and Herculean struggle. If the world is ugly and wretched, however, renunciation is really the easy way out. Somebody who pushes away a plate of something delicious is disciplined, whereas someone who pushes away a plate of rancid filth has nothing to brag about. Modern society has become so thoroughly unappetizing that there is no longer anything heroic about separating oneself from it. Escape is a necessity. Those who turn their backs on the modern world are more like refugees escaping from a warzone than enlightened saints. No one is going to be impressed because you refused to eat your cockroaches. [*ETIS* 199]

39. The modern clergy believe they can bring man closer to Christ by insisting on Christ's humanity, neglecting the fact that we do not trust in Christ because he is man, but because he is God.

Gómez Dávila constantly returns to the theme of what Christianity has abandoned or lost in its ongoing attempt to stay relevant in a world that is fundamentally incompatible with its teachings. In order to appeal to the worst in man, the Church can only present what is worst in Christ. And yet a Christianity that preaches the worship of a man, whether or not that man is Christ, can be no true religion. To seek to lure man to the Church by preaching social justice and humanism is to undermine the most central premise of Christianity: the divinity of Christ. Deprived of his divine status, what in Christ would remain that is worthy of our worship or faith? [*ETIS* 472]

40. **To suppress specific liturgies is to suppress specific truths. To fell sacred groves is to erase divine footprints.**

It is bad enough that the Second Vatican Council abolished so much in the liturgies which had produced both a symbolic richness unparalleled in the West and a sense of awe and beauty. Worse still that in doing so, the Church fundamentally altered the focus and purpose of religious worship. In the absence of the ritual and supernatural aspects of Christianity, the Church leaves the nonrational world of sacred mystery and enters the anthropocentric world of logic and reason. Any attempt to make religion more palatable to modern man undermines the very meaning of religion. In this context, what could be a more suitable task for the Church than addressing worldly problems and promoting social justice or some trivial ethical system? Thus, the Church loses its mysticism and becomes an essentially irreligious institution. The pagan nemeton indicated more than a connection to the natural world—its existence demonstrated an orientation toward the sacred outside of and explicitly *opposed to* the human world. [*ETIS* 297]

41. **From an encounter with the gods of the underworld, we must take care lest we return as madmen.**

Here a nod might be seen to Nietzsche's dictum from *Beyond Good and Evil*:

> He who fights with monsters should look to it that he himself does not become a monster. And when you gaze long into an abyss the abyss also gazes into you. (146)

That we accept, like C. G. Jung, the need for a confrontation with the subterranean gods does not mean that we are blind to the risks. We venture into the shadowy realm of the underworld because we understand that these demonic forces have the power to destroy us and that our only hopes lies in facing them, vanquishing them, and integrating them. For Gómez Dávila, of course, like Eliade, this sense of integration comes through Christ. This is the same type of tolerance for paganism as a precursor to Christianity that can be seen even among Catholics like Cardinal Newman and G. K. Chesterton. Jung was less convinced that the fate of the underworld gods was to be subsumed and perfected within Christ. In either case, at stake in this confrontation is sanity and the soul itself. To deny the darker forces allows them to grow in power and subtly influence us. To challenge them we risk defeat and being swallowed by the abyss. [*ETIS* 314]

42. **The Christian has nothing to lose in a catastrophe.**

Both the devotee of progress and the nihilist fear catastrophe—the former because it spoils his pretension to godhood, and the latter because it presents itself as purposeless and arbitrary suffering. For one who accepts that mankind can never fully understand or control the destiny of the cosmos, however, catastrophe occurs as what it really is: an overturning and the coming of change. If the movements of the world are directed by the guiding hand of the Creator, we must be attentive to that which catastrophe offers us. If we trust in the will of God or the gods, we can see that things happen as they must, no matter how terrible they may seem. As Montaigne wrote, paraphrasing

Plato: "Good men, whether in life or after death, have no cause to fear the gods" (332). [*ETIS* 97]

43. **In this age when every famous site is desecrated by hordes of tourists, the only way for a reverent pilgrim to honor a sacred shrine is simply not to go there.**

In a modern world, where everything is profaned and all understanding of the sacred has been lost, the act of pilgrimage becomes devoid of meaning. The incredible ease and even comfort with which one travels has meant that even the holiest site can be but one destination among others. Today Lourdes, tomorrow Santiago—all reached in the luxury of passenger aircrafts and private automobiles. Snap a few photos, have a good meal, and move on to the next place of interest. It is impossible to imagine any shrine remaining in the world today that is not littered with fast-food wrappers, where the air is not deafened by the voices of irreverent tongues shouting into their cell phones. In general, it seems that modern man is really only likely to be on the path toward God when he stays put. [*ETIS* 89]

44. **Progress is the calamity God has chosen for us.**

The notion of progress was born in the moment when cyclical time was replaced by linear time. Suddenly, the natural laws of birth, growth, decay, death and subsequent rebirth were replaced by the heretical idea that history moves inevitably toward completion and perfection. Did this idea begin with Christianity and the promise of the Second Coming? Did it begin with the natural scientists of the Renaissance, who envisioned a cosmos governed by perceptible and manipulatable laws, which could be organized in favor of the betterment of the human race? Or the revolutionaries of the Enlightenment, who saw in the notion of liberty the capacity to build a utopian society? Perhaps progress was the punishment for breaking with tradition and the sacred. As humanity turns away from God, He sends us this pernicious ideology that now destroys the world and humanity. Progress, and the doom it brings, was always our destiny. [*ETIS* 82]

45. **Christianity does not deny the splendor of the world, but rather invites us to search for its origin, to ascend toward its loftiest heights.**

Many of the most powerful arguments against Christianity come down to the matter of denying the world. To say that Christianity envisions a world created *ex nihilo*, utterly separated from the divinity of God, is, of course, not wholly unreasonable. Nevertheless, the beauty of the world is sacred and thus may be seen as emanating from the divine. The presence of God can be perceived in the perfect geometry of the snowflake, or in the whispering of the wind in the leaves, or in the spectacular glory of Blake's tiger, prowling through the dark woods, pulsing with the fearsome light and power of its creator. Here, then, Christianity is the greatest affirmation of the world, rather than its denial. [*ETIS* 73]

46. **Spiritual maturity begins when we no longer feel ourselves responsible for managing the world.**

It is no coincidence that the age of materialism holds two truths above all: that the spiritual beliefs of the past are nothing but superstition, and that the ideal society can be created through proper administration. Of course, these two premises are complementary. If the spiritual world is denied its agency, then what is left but for the world to be governed by an empire of bureaucrats? In the absence of the spirit, life and society both appear to be nothing but a matter of balancing a ledger.

The modern experience of life, reduced to columns indicating nothing more profound than surplus or deficit, can be arranged more or less efficiently. In the end, the history of the past several hundred years appears to prove nothing if not that the more good humanity tries to do, the more catastrophic the outcome. The world is well cared for; it is the soul of humanity that requires healing. Until this is achieved there will be no solution in society or the world that will count for anything. [*ETIS* 26]

III
Politics and Education

1. **Education does not cure stupidity; it arms it.**

As Alexander Pope observed in his poem *An Essay on Criticism* (1711), a small amount of learning is a dangerous thing. No education at all is infinitely preferable to a poor or incomplete one. It is increasingly difficult to receive a proper education in modern society because, among other reasons, we misunderstand the purpose of education. As Montaigne writes: "Learning is a great ornament," but

> in low and menial hands it is not properly employed. It takes much more pride in lending its powers to the conduct of war, to the ruling of a people, to cultivating the friendship of a prince or a foreign nation, than in devoting itself to the composition of a dialectical argument, or in arguing an appeal, or in prescribing a packet of pills. (54)

Education, in other words, should not be motivated by profit, unless the profit we gain is to become wiser and better. If wisdom is not the goal of education, then we should not be surprised to be surrounded by so many millions of educated fools. Cicero reminds us that "Instruction in right living, the most fruitful of all the arts, is to be gained by life itself rather than by study" (cited in Montaigne, 75). If a man does not know how to live, education will not save him and there are few arts as neglected and undervalued in modern society as the art of living. [*ETIS* 328]

2. **No diploma can cure an illiteracy of the soul.**

There are few better examples to illustrate the stupidity of modern education than the life of Michel de Montaigne. This unfathomably brilliant man's father, after searching for the most perfect means of educating his child and thereby discovering how little modern education was worth, determined that his son's education should solely consist of the study of Latin. Montaigne was raised speaking only Latin and was six years old before he learned a single word in French. Since Latin was his mother tongue, Montaigne naturally read the works of classical antiquity. They were the only books that he could read. Of any other imaginable subject, he was completely ignorant. Even in his forties, when he wrote his essays, he confesses:

> I know there is a science of medicine, one of jurisprudence, and four divisions of mathematics, and also roughly what their purposes are. I know too, perhaps, how much the sciences in general have contributed to our lives. But as for plunging any deeper, or for biting my nails over the study of Aristotle, the monarch of modern learning, or stoutly pursuing any particular branch of knowledge, that I have never done. Nor is there any art of which I could sketch even the elementary outlines. There is no child in the middle forms who cannot lay claim to more learning than I, who am incapable of examining him in his first lessons. (49)

Nevertheless, Montaigne's observations on human nature are unlikely to be surpassed in their accuracy and insight. Today's diplomas guarantee that the recipient has successfully consumed and regurgitated a sufficient number of facts and ideas and that is all. A modern general education ensures nothing more than that the pupil will have nothing meaningful to say about anything. [*ETIS* 262]

3. **If one's goal is merely to provide an increasing number of goods**

to an increasing number of people, without being concerned with the quality of those people, or those goods, then capitalism is the perfect solution.

The vast majority of today's anti-capitalists fail to recognize that capitalism is, in fact, the most suitable system to accommodate their ideology. The egalitarian impulse of John Stuart Mill and others—who sought to organize society according to a simple calculus of measurable, material needs—culminates in contemporary capitalism. The truth is that capitalism gives people what they want and therein lies its greatest crime. Modern egalitarian society is not motivated by creating better, wiser, happier people, but by providing them with things. To adapt a phrase from Joseph de Maistre, everyone gets the society they deserve. [*ETIS* 326]

4. **Individualism is not the antithesis of totalitarianism, but a condition of it.**
Totalitarianism and hierarchy, on the other hand, are the endpoints of opposing movements.

The opposite of totalitarianism is not a society made up of millions of isolated individuals selfishly pursuing their own whims and desires. On the contrary, totalitarianism is a society in which the selfish whims and desires of millions of isolated individuals are manipulated so as to shape them into an undifferentiated mass. The opposite of totalitarianism is a society in which the individual belongs to and represents an order that is more important than his own whims and desires. The opposite of totalitarianism is an integrated society in which every member plays his role. It is, in short, a hierarchical one. [*ETIS* 321]

5. **After having been, in the last century, the instrument of**

political radicalism, universal suffrage is becoming, as Tocqueville anticipated, a conservative mechanism.

The French Revolution quickly demonstrated how egalitarianism leads to repression. The new constitution was unconditional and therefore made enemies of everything it could not absorb. All dissent or plurality of opinion was recast as treason. In the words of Mirabeau: "Our nation of apes with parrots' voices!" (cited in Burckhardt, 247). Even the voice of one as wise as Tocqueville is lost amidst the deafening clamor of thoughtless consensus. In the aftermath of the Revolution, all institutions that existed outside of the egalitarian state were obliterated: the Church, guilds and associations, charitable and educational organizations, and so on and so forth. The overall effect of the Revolution was, in Burckhardt's phrase, a "general pulverization" (247). Little has changed in this regard. The champions of egalitarianism today are no less puritanical than the *philosophes* and Revolutionaries of the eighteenth century. [*ETIS* 468]

6. **Each day we demand more from society so that we can demand less from ourselves.**

The individual in modern society, atomized and disconnected from community or class, is necessarily fragile and helpless. Deprived of that from which he may derive wisdom or strength, he sees himself in need of rescuing and not without reason. He no longer knows how to care for himself, what to think, or how to act. As an isolated individual, man is an empty shell. Society at large is only too happy to fill the void. Society tells us how to think and how to act because we no longer trust ourselves. Thus conditioned, the modern individual becomes weaker and weaker, while his reliance on society becomes greater and greater. [*ETIS* 228]

7. **On the barren steppe the individual finds no protection from the hostility of nature, nor in an egalitarian society does he find protection from the hostility of man.**

Egalitarian society, which refuses to honor any law or principle other than egalitarianism itself, is fundamentally inhospitable to man. As Maistre observes: "All bonds of society were loosed, and the most dangerous passions became even more venomous" (152). Egalitarianism can only conceive of bonds as repressive, and fails to see that they connect us to each other through loyalty, virtue, and community. Even Voltaire, who was made into a hero of the French Revolution, saw how democracy leads to the tyranny of the vicious and hateful masses. In a letter to Frederick the Great of Prussia, he writes: "When I supplicated you to be the restorer of the beaux-arts of Greece, my prayer did not go so far as to implore you to restore Athenian democracy: I do not like the government of the rabble" (cited in Maistre, 268). Indeed, the example of Athens is illustrative. Popular opinion did not serve her well and must be seen to have caused her considerable harm. Maistre notes:

> Aristides and Cimon were banished; Themistocles and Timothy died in exile; Socrates and Phocion drank the hemlock. Athens did not spare one of its great men. (268)

We should require no greater evidence as to the dangers of democracy than the abundant crimes of history that were sanctioned and celebrated by the masses. [*ETIS* 233]

8. **Vulgarity is not a product of the masses, but a byproduct of bourgeois prosperity.**

True vulgarity is not what is found among the uneducated and unsophisticated poor, but rather among the prosperous middle class, which believes that money is the only thing that matters. In fact, in modern society, it is only among the poor that one finds some vestigial attachment to tradition, religion, or virtue. In the words of Lactantius: "The common people are wiser because they are no wiser than they need to be" (cited in Montaigne, 223). The man of the bourgeoisie must always pretend to be more than he is. This is the essence of vulgarity. [*ETIS* 257]

9. **"Finding himself," for modern man, means dissolving himself in a collective identity.**

In the modern world the path of self-knowledge inevitably leads to delusion. Freedom of thought and expression results in our increasing identification with restrictive and limited groups, which themselves enslave us. *I am who I am because I belong to this identity*, modern man declares. Little does he realize that he has put himself in a box and learned nothing about himself whatsoever. Of course, capitalism greatly appreciates the willingness with which individuals enthusiastically reduce themselves to categories. It is much easier to rule a group of people who force themselves to think and act the same way because they believe it is their identity. [*ETIS* 281]

10. **Liberty is the term most employed without anyone knowing what it means.**

It is simultaneously true that everyone loves liberty and that everyone has a different understanding of what it means. For the revolutionaries of 1789 it meant exchanging the power of the monarch for the power of a murderous bureaucratic state. For Maistre it meant being bound by the flexible chains of the Supreme Being. For the contemporary American it means being able to choose whom he may freely oppress and by whom he may in turn be oppressed. If one thing is clear, it is that anything can be done in the name of liberty. [*ETIS* 361]

11. **Men disagree not because they think differently, but because they do not think at all.**

Ultimately, no matter their differences, thinking people will always find much to agree upon. The fool, on the other hand, will always find something to disagree about because his opinions are not the product of any kind of consideration but merely his unexplored assumptions and emotional reactions. Wisdom consists in discerning what is true, which is always the same regardless of superficial differences. [*ETIS* 117]

12. **Essentially, the revolutionary is a man who does not suspect that humanity is capable of acting against itself.**

The Marxist, the socialist, is essentially one who sees the source of humanity's suffering in an external system that has been imposed upon it. It is not inaccurate to suggest that capitalism or industrialism have taken on a life of their own, which predetermine the actions of the human individuals that live within such a system. What this perspective ignores, however, is the fact that modern man has been given the power to consistently, and as a rule, act against his own interests. As the unalterable laws and truths are subjected to human interpretation and eroded, man gains the freedom to choose and it is a mistake not to assume that the world he now inhabits is the product of that choice. It is not a coincidence that the advent of the modern world was immediately preceded by the Protestant Reformation, which taught that man should be his own master and judge. [*ETIS* 137]

13. **Only the imbecile never feels like he is collaborating with his enemies.**

Ideological purity under any circumstances is an indication of weakness of thought. It demonstrates that one is unable to maintain distinctions. On some level, rigidly clinging to one's principles in this modern world is foolishness. All is corrupted, all is profaned. While staying true to one's soul, nevertheless, one must inevitably walk amongst the wretchedness and squalor of this world. And so walking, one may find unexpected fellow travelers. How can modern man live without tacitly lending his support to that which he despises? [*ETIS* 111]

14. **The proletarian only hates the bourgeois because of the economic difficulty of emulating him.**

There certainly may have been a time in the recent past when the proletariat and the bourgeoisie were enemies, though now it seems like the former has largely given up his hostility toward the latter in favor of admiration. But we can say that throughout the history of the proletariat, the real thing a proletarian hated about the bourgeoisie was that he was poor while the other was rich. The proletarian resents the fact that he is not the one with the office job, the two cars, the suburban home, the big TV, and so on and so forth. When it comes down to it, the proletarian is just a frustrated member of the bourgeoisie. Leftism will never represent anything more meaningful unless it stops trying to simply raise the poor to the condition of the rich—a condition, incidentally, which the Jesus of the gospels could not be more clear about condemning. [*ETIS* 78]

15. **The putrefaction of modern civilization can only be doubted in an underdeveloped country.**

It is telling that the only people who still believe in the fantasy of the American dream don't live here. America only seems like the land of promise to people who live somewhere else. Once they arrive, they quickly realize their mistake. God forbid, if they succeed in joining the ranks of the middle class, they find their lives dominated by meaningless tedium and soullessness. And those so-called underdeveloped nations, in their attempts to modernize, will discover too late that they are destroying themselves. Only those who live in First World nations, who see the price of their prosperity, understand how little they have gained. [*ETIS* 167]

16. The concept of "divine right" limited the monarch; the "mandate of the people" represents an unconditional form of absolutism.

One of the many errors in modern thinking, which takes for granted that any previous form of society must have been inferior, lies in assuming that the monarch wielded absolute power. The president or prime minister, modern man believes, is held accountable through checks and balances to his power. In fact, the reverse is the case. The monarch was supremely limited in his power not only by the complementary roles of the aristocracy and the Church, but more importantly, by the nature of the source of his authority. To rule by divine right does not mean the monarch can do as he pleases. It means that his power is entirely subject to the will of God. This indicates both the necessity for the monarch to behave according to a set of higher laws and the possibility for God to withdraw favor for the monarch if he fails to properly adhere to these laws. Democracy, on the other hand, acknowledges no power or law beyond the will of the people. If the people or their elected representatives have made a decision, there is no basis for questioning that decision. It does not matter if it was right or wrong; it is what the people have chosen. [*ETIS* 349]

17. **Order paralyzes. Disorder creates upheavals. The miracle of feudalism was to integrate disorder within an all-inclusive sense of order.**

In essence, the feudal system allowed for power to be distributed broadly in society. Multiple sources of authority were nevertheless held in balance. The aristocracy, the Church, the peasantry, and the sovereign consistently struggled against each other for power, but none of them were able to concentrate that power to the extent that they were able to utterly dominate the others. As Burckhardt observed, the collapse of feudalism and the triumph of the modern state created the conditions for total domination in society. It is no coincidence that the first modern states were those of the Italian tyrants. The modern state is defined by the need for centralization to the extent that it cannot allow any other power to exist elsewhere. Institutions like the Church and the aristocracy are reduced to symbolic or honorary status. The power and authority of the individual resigns completely. As the power of any agent outside the state diminishes, the state becomes the sole arbiter. Laws and rights are defined exclusively by the state and are only conferred according to the will of the state. As the state gives, the state can take away. [*ETIS* 264]

18. **The state grows by the same degree that the individual diminishes.**

Maistre constantly draws our attention to ancient Sparta as an example of a society in which social cohesion eliminated the need for legislation. To paraphrase the Daoist sages of the *Daodejing*, laws are only needed once mankind has become lawless. Righteousness can only exist where virtue has already been forgotten. Where the individual is weak, decrepit, and helpless, the state is vigorous and powerful. The modern democrat hopes to make man good by strengthening the state. If we have enough laws, and the right kind of laws, it will force individuals to make the right decisions. But if any desirable qualities in humanity are only the product of being correctly administered and coerced by the state, what is their value? Maistre again: to only give men rights really gives them nothing at all. [*ETIS* 28]

19. **The sinister uniformity that threatens us will not be imposed by design, but by a standardizing process of economic and social conditioning.**

The most oppressive forms of domination in modern society are not the malevolent schemes and stratagems of the wicked elites; rather, they are often the product of apparently benign systems that determine our quotidian lives and routines. It is always easier to point the finger at some shadowy entity that is secretly pulling the strings than to acknowledge the countless ways that we actively become the instrument of our own oppression. The proliferation of conspiracy theories at the present moment demonstrates how enthusiastically people seek to construct narratives that will allow them to abdicate all agency and responsibility. [*ETIS* 462]

20. **There is only one choice at the end of this century: Eastern barracks or Western brothel.**

Increasingly, the only plausible visions of society presented to us at the late stage of this dark age are the coercive inhuman administration of totalitarianism in the East and the meaningless hedonism and degeneracy of liberalism in the West. We are caught between two equally intolerable images of society. [*ETIS* 190]

21. **The appearance of nationalism in any nation indicates that its**

originality is dying.

Nationalism is the clearest indication that the dynamic forces that animated a culture have been exhausted. Great cultures degenerate into nations, which is the same thing as to say that the state represents the erosion and bankruptcy of the communal or the individual will. The vitality of ancient Celtic culture was such that for more than a thousand years, it resisted the kind of stagnation that leads to state formation. While cultures and communities derive their motivations from an internal guiding principle, the state or the nation is only motivated by the accumulation of power. Thus, militarism becomes a defining characteristic of the nation and the latter cannot exist without the former. By the same token, internally, the nation is defined by the necessity toward uniformity and agglomeration, which it achieves by ruthlessly crushing dissent and diversity. The national will, which is certainly not the same thing as the will of the people, is the almighty sovereign of this world. [*ETIS* 191]

22. **Modern society has the luxury of permitting everyone to say what they want because everyone in this society basically thinks the same thing.**

As we are beginning to see in the benign and enlightened democratic societies of the West, freedom of speech really only exists as long as nobody says anything that those in power don't want to hear. As long as there is total unanimity, everyone is allowed to speak as they like. But on the rare occasions when someone actually thinks differently from the masses, he will soon find himself silenced. Just as Francis Fukuyama mistakenly assumed that the triumph of neoliberal capitalism and Western democratic values had eliminated all global opposition, freedom of speech is predicated on the false notion that nobody could possibly disagree with the values of this society. To the extent that dissenting opinions have begun to emerge, the majority and those in power respond with shock. We are so used to being presented with so-called new or opposing ideas that nevertheless perpetuate the status quo, when we hear a genuinely dissenting opinion we are confused and generally feel like somehow the speaker is not playing according to the rules. [*ETIS* 63]

23. **Even the most extreme version of the Right seems to me too far to the Left.**

Is there any manifestation of the Right that fundamentally rejects the modern deification of man and his reason? Is there any tendency we could call "right wing" that seeks the absolute destruction of techno-industrial society? Does any right-wing platform actually oppose the authority of the state? Is there any sense of modern politics that does not affirm capitalism as the basis for that society? Modern politics, in any of its various guises, is progressive. For Gómez Dávila, the entire political arena is already blasphemous. Even the religious fundamentalists seek to bring God into the realm of petty worldly concerns. The only versions of Left and Right that would have any significance or value would be ones that completely abandon politics. [*ETIS* 209]

24. **The three hypostases of egoism are: individualism, nationalism, collectivism. The democratic trinity.**

There has been much conflation of egoism and individualism, but the latter is not the only form which the former may take. Faith in the nation-state or in the collective is merely a broader application of egoism. There is an assumption that democracy and individualism are contrary forces. But really democracy itself, in its most basic sense, is an egoism extended to humanity as a whole. In democracy it is not merely the individual, the nation-state, or the collective that is sovereign and autonomous, but the entire society and humanity at large. The basis for this egoism is the postulate that mankind is capable of directing its own course and is qualified to both judge itself and create its own meaning. What could be more selfish and callous than to seek to achieve a world where mankind is king? [*ETIS* 130]

25. **If the Europeans renounce their particularities in order to create the "good European," we fear they will have only succeeded in creating another American.**

In a misguided attempt to avoid a repetition of the horrors the twentieth century, the new liberal European order attempts to eliminate the distinct character of European communities. Instead of cultures, there will only be economic markets. The United States is clearly the best example of this. The tremendous diversity of American society is reduced to anonymous uniformity by capitalism and techno-industrialism. And Europe seems to be heading in the same direction. The melting pot analogy, as it turns out, is more apt than it might seem. Ingredients in a pot will eventually dissolve and become indistinguishable from one another, leaving one with a flavorless mush. Multiculturalism is not the problem, as long as differences and particularities are honored and respected. [*ETIS* 162]

26. **A "classless society" is one where there is neither aristocrat nor common man, where only the bourgeois can move about freely.**

The dream of the leftist, if it ever came to pass, would be the most banal nightmare. Universal emancipation would lead directly to universal degradation. The aristocrat has, of course, long since ceased to exist. The greater crime of a classless society would be that committed against the common people, devaluing their traditions and culture, and insisting that they join the ranks of the lifeless bourgeoisie. Vibrant working-class communities, according to the pitiless logic of leftism, should be leveled and replaced by anonymous suburban neighborhoods filled with two-car garages and individual yards surrounded by white picket fences. The greatest irony of leftism is that it claims to represent and defend the poor, while despising them and everything about their lives. [*ETIS* 283]

27. **Modern man believes he is surrounded by a multiplicity of opinions, but what rules today is a suffocating unanimity.**

Today's political commentators lament what they perceive as the "divisiveness" of modern society. We hear so much about how society has become polarized and how disagreements have become irresolvable. If only, the pundits wail, we could learn how to better empathize with the other and come to an agreement! What is shocking in this complaint is how it completely fails to recognize the overwhelming consensus found in modern society. Whatever political squabbles divide the people, they are shallow and trivial compared to the enormity of what they implicitly agree upon. Fundamentally, no one in this society has any disagreement whatsoever about the correct way to live and about the assumptions that govern our lives. There is no statistically meaningful portion of the population that questions the role of technology in our lives, or industrial production, or capitalism, or urbanism, or progress, or nationalism, or the fundamental nature of man's existence. [*ETIS* 459]

28. **It is not enough for the citizen to passively submit; the modern state requires accomplices.**

Ultimately, the reign of the modern world would be less oppressive if its methods were purely and nakedly coercive. Submission, as it turns out, is not the least desirable condition. It is far easier to convince man to do evil on his own behalf than to force him to do so externally. In the world of the modern state, the citizen is both prisoner and prison warden. The greater license he is given to oppress, the greater oppression he will turn upon himself. The citizen of the modern state enthusiastically applies to become policeman and bureaucrat. Thus, he does not only suffer under a system that is harmful to him, he takes an active role in its perpetuation. Who is to blame for the ills of modern society? Unquestionably, it is every single member of that society. Those with the most power suffer from its wickedness, no less than those who are the most wretched. In this regard, Marx was absolutely correct that those who wield the power of capital at the highest levels are by no means immune to its controlling influence. They are slaves just as much as the rest of us. And they are no more able to act differently than we are. No one person or class or institution holds power. In fact, it becomes more and more clear that in contemporary modern society, no one at all is in charge of anything. Nothing and nobody reigns, and all are slaves and more impoverished for it. [*ETIS* 108]

29. **It would be easier to resolve modern problems, if, for example, it were possible to maintain the utopian fantasy that the production of plastic objects is due only to the manufacturer's commercial greed, and not the idiotic enthusiasm of the consumer.**

In general, the chief error of the leftist is to assume that the horrors of capitalism are exclusively the product of the greed of the capitalist. The leftists imagine that the capitalist functions as the feudal lord, the aristocrat, or the monarch, wielding total power and imposing it on everyone else from the top down. If only they were right! All that would be needed if such were the case is the simplest possible course of action. Unfortunately, this fantasy neglects the sad truth that those who suffer under capitalism contribute to and perpetuate it with a fanaticism that equals or exceeds their supposed oppressors.

The endless stream of products and gadgets which the capitalist produces are gleefully consumed by the people. They desire nothing more than to be sold the most worthless rubbish and to devour it like an animal licking up its own vomit. Capitalist greed can thus only ever be a portion of the problem, but it is invariably the one that leftists and social reformers make primary. It is always easier to lay the blame elsewhere. [*ETIS* 155]

30. **In societies where everybody believes they are equal, the unavoidable superiority of some makes the rest feel like failures. Conversely, in societies where inequality is normal, each person settles into his own sense of unique difference, without being compelled to compare himself to others, or even being able to contemplate the possibility. Only a hierarchical structure can be compassionate toward the mediocre and the meek.**

Has man's resentment and envy been lessened or intensified by his insistence upon the value of equality? If all are meant to be equal and yet inequality appears to be universal, how is anyone expected to be content with themselves? Certainly, much of the blame for this lies on capitalism. If man's worth is judged exclusively by his economic means, but his ability to accumulate wealth is determined by factors beyond his control, then he can only ever be dissatisfied. In ages past, on the other hand, power, wealth, and nobility were conferred by birth. One could never aspire to the state of another and all played a vital role. Those who were strong were recognized as such, along with the attendant obligations placed upon strength, and those who were weak were accepted as being in need of protection and support. The "leveling of the playing field" has simply meant that every member of society fights tooth and nail against all others, and some with enormous advantages, which predispose them to always win the rigged game. [*ETIS* 138]

31. **Capitalist society enriched itself by combining the ignorance of the shrewd manager, who tells people what to do, with the science of the dimwitted engineer, who gets things done. Socialism presumes to enrich itself by entrusting the management to the engineer.**

A society is bad enough in which power lies in the hands of one who knows nothing other than how to direct the hands of one who is skilled in labor. But why should we assume that the situation would be improved by putting the power to direct and manage into the hands of one who knows nothing other than how to labor? For Gómez Dávila, the aristocracy was uniquely qualified to rule, not because of any inherent superiority, but because it allowed for the dissemination of an inherited training regimen. Needless to say, the capitalist CEO has nothing in common with the aristocrat other than his wealth. Equality does not so much provide increased opportunities as much as it makes the members of a society interchangeable and thus equally disposable. The impulse of the socialist, at root, is erroneously to assume that all members of society should be capable of fulfilling the role of any other. Such a situation would surely lead to a suffocating uniformity in which an enormous proportion of the tasks of mankind would be done poorly. [*ETIS* 195]

32. **The world is not so bad considering those who govern it.**

As bad as things in modern society are, they should, by all rights, be much worse. There is everywhere the assumption that one's enemies in society are devious and clever, that they execute nefarious schemes, and perpetrate vast conspiracies. The truth—which is both fortunate and unfortunate—is that there is only confusion and stupidity. It flatters us to think our enemies powerful and wise. On the other hand, our struggles are trivialized when we recognize that our foes are only as misguided and foolish as ourselves. In the words of Frederick the Great of Prussia: "When I think that a fool, an imbecile like St. Ignatius found a dozen proselytes to follow him, and that I could not find three philosophers, I have been tempted to believe that reason is good for nothing" (cited in Maistre, 218). When we see how little human action is motivated by reason, even among the most powerful, when we see how stupid and blind are the leaders of the world, it is frankly shocking that society functions at all. [*ETIS* 409]

33. **The tragedy of the Left is to diagnose the malady correctly, but to aggravate it with its therapy.**

One of the central tenets of philosophical Daoism is the notion that action is generally more harmful than inaction. As man is limited both in his understanding of the world and in his self-understanding; his actions inevitably produce undesirable consequences. Man is capable of acting in the world, but he is not capable of understanding what those actions will lead to. The failures of the Left over the last century demonstrate this clearly. The leftist is by no means incorrect in his assessment of the problems of the modern world, but he insists that he knows how to address them. Worse still, he has acted upon these conclusions and, more often than not, has increased the suffering he sought to eliminate. Capitalism is unquestionably horrific and devastating beyond measure, but the global struggles of the Left have neither succeeded in diminishing the power of capitalism, nor in putting forward an alternative that is in any way preferable to it. [*ETIS* 141]

34. **Today's conservatives are nothing more than liberals who have been mistreated by democracy.**

For the last several decades there has been nothing to distinguish the conservative from the liberal except for the fact that public opinion has gone against him. Now there seems to be a resurgence of conservative populism and so the pendulum swings back. Liberal and conservative fight for popular approval and that is the sum total of their political visions. The politics of the contemporary world is a politics of resentment. Both sides are alike as victims of the despotism of the masses, but in either case we really see very little of conservatism or liberalism, only a shameless and universal pandering. Partisans on both sides are inclined to place the fault for their defeat on the elected officials who are the ostensible victors, but it is always the ravening masses that create these figureheads. No matter what, in democracy it is the ignorant and hysterical who triumph. [*ETIS* 211]

35. **It is not a coincidence that revolutions are succeeded by bureaucracies. Revolutions are the bloody births of bureaucracies.**

To tear down an old order, one must replace it with another. Destruction is an easy thing for man. To create something beautiful and meaningful is a more laborious task. The impulse of the revolutionary is to destroy; he knows nothing of creation. Furthermore, he finds that once he has executed the last enemy of the revolution, he has no idea how to implement his ideals. Of course, we understand that this is because there is truly no new structure available to him. He can only ever reconstruct the very system he has destroyed. Therefore when the dust settles and the fighting is over, the contribution of the revolutionary is at an end and the task falls to that quintessential figure of the modern world: the bureaucrat. What does it matter whether the head of a bureaucracy is the Chairman of the People, the chairman of the board, or the democratically elected representative. The true sovereign power in the modern world is the petty clerk. [*ETIS* 175]

36. **When we hear the final chords of a national anthem, we know for sure that someone has just uttered a bunch of nonsense.**

The modern nation state, as a product of the ever-increasing influence of the bourgeoisie on society, can make no legitimate claim to authority. In the absence of monarchs and aristocratic clans trained in statecraft and rule, the nation becomes nothing more than the tool of bureaucrats and positivists. Nationalism can only ever celebrate the victory of mediocrity. [*ETIS* 156]

37. **Democratic elections merely decide whom it is permitted to legally oppress.**

Putting the power to choose into the hands of the people does not ensure freedom or the absence of oppression; it guarantees that those whom the people are convinced to hate will have no protection under the law. In the context of the United States, the practice of oppressing minorities is thoroughly entrenched within the legal system. Even when laws exist that are supposed to prevent oppression, they are neglected by an indifferent public and corrupt institutions. The criminal forms of oppression and viciousness are overwhelmingly eclipsed by those that democratic societies sanction. To adapt a phrase from Maistre: it is not men that direct the course of democracy; it is democracy, understood here as the despotism of the masses, that directs men. The contemporary rise of populism makes this abundantly clear. Caught up in the fervor, those who make up these movements become instruments of them. As Maistre observed about the French Revolution, divine providence may utilize even the most repulsive means to castigate us. The same applies to democracy. [*ETIS* 315]

38. **Either man has rights, or the people are sovereign.**
The simultaneous assertion of these two mutually exclusive theses is what is called liberalism.

Modern liberal democracy is founded upon a fundamental incoherence around rights and sovereignty. In essence, the problem is this: if rights are inalienable, if all men possess certain rights no matter what, then they are beyond all authority, including the sovereignty of the people, but if rights are dependent upon a sovereign entity to declare and enforce them, then they are politically contingent, and man may frequently find that he does not in fact possess them at all. If the people are ultimately sovereign, does that mean they have the power to take rights away? If so, those rights must be seen to count for very little. As Maistre writes:

> They say that the people are sovereign; but over whom? Over themselves, apparently. The people are, therefore, subject. There is surely some equivocation here if not an error, for the people who command are not the people who obey. (165) [*ETIS* 360]

39. **The separation of Church and State may suit the Church, but it is fatal for the State because it is thereby reduced to pure Machiavellianism.**

Without being tethered to the State, the Church may focus more diligently upon its true purpose: the spiritual cultivation of humanity. We see this, for instance, in the Eastern church, which was always exempted from political considerations and never became a worldly power. Once the state becomes the sole authority in society, however, and is no longer answerable to any other, its cruelty and opportunism cannot be restrained. The old model of throne and altar, we might say, preserved order and balance by providing a necessary counter to the power of the state. In the modern world, the state is all. [*ETIS* 402]

40. Modern liberalism no longer defends any of the "rights of man" except the right to consume.

How far has the revolutionary dream of democratic liberty fallen! As long as man believes that he possesses rights, he does not even notice or care when they are stripped away from him. Modern democracy affirms the political vision of man as a rights-bearing entity, even as it ensures that he will not profit from them in any way. Does the fact that man legally possesses this or that right mean that he is able to benefit from what that right supposedly entitles him to? Clearly not. He may have rights, but he has little else, and profits from those rights not at all. He has liberty, but no food or home. He has equality, but no money or power. As the truth of this fantasy becomes clear, we begin to understand that we have no rights at all, other than the right to live as slaves. In the words of Maistre: "[I]f your offices do not elevate those who possess them, do not boast of giving them to everyone, for you shall not give them anything." Similarly, Karl Jaspers writes:

> [T]he general fellowship of our human situation has been rendered even more dubious than before, inasmuch as, though the old ties of caste have been loosened, a new restriction of the individual to some prescribed status in the sociological machinery has become manifest. Less than ever, perhaps, is it possible for a man to transcend the limitations imposed by his social origins. (*Man in the Modern Age*, 25)

Modern man, for all his liberty, is the most fundamentally unfree individual in human history.

41. The leftist obviously refuses to accept that the foundational principles of leftist thought are derived from the conclusions of bourgeois thought.

The class that originally developed the ideas to which the leftist subscribes is the same one that he struggles against now. The core principles of socialism—democracy, equality, and liberty—were first articulated by the bourgeoisie. And it is precisely these ideas that enabled the rise of capitalism. The contemporary leftist would be shocked and horrified to find, upon meeting with an early capitalist, that his enemy agreed entirely with his values. Both are invested in increasing the power of the state as the safeguard of rights and freedoms, and, above all, both agree in their hatred for the reactionary. [*ETIS* 362]

42. **One speaks of a society of consumption in order to conceal the fact that, since production is the progressive ideal, one is really dealing with a society of productivity.**

The modern progressive reformer is quick to criticize the consumption habits of society, and for good reason. Consumerism is clearly an enormous part of the problem, but it is not the only problem and may ultimately not even be the primary problem of modern industrial society. For this we must look deeper into the principles of the modern world at its core. The vision that is universally shared by the capitalist and the socialist, the progressive and the conservative, is one that prioritizes productivity above all else. Once again, even among socialists, Marx was unique in understanding that the mode of distributing goods was of secondary importance compared to the impact made by the dehumanizing processes of production. The source of the crisis lies in production, which necessitates the creation of demand. Like the other most deeply held modern convictions, however, society cannot bear to question the value of production itself. [*ETIS* 448]

43. **There are two equally erroneous attitudes toward Marxism: disdaining what it teaches and believing what it promises.**

The contemporary conservative makes at least one fatal mistake: he refuses to accept that capitalism is a primary source of the degradation of the modern world. Capitalism, as the economic expression of the bourgeois mentality, lies at the very heart of modernity. The rejection of capitalism is a defining principle in the reactionary position. There is likewise no question that Marx was the most brilliant critic and analyst of capitalism. If the conservative's mistake is to fail to recognize that capitalism is his enemy and that Marxism can help him understand that fact, the leftist's mistake is to think that the solutions and predictions of the Marxists have any truth or value. There is no shortage of accurate diagnoses, the problem is when we assume that diagnosis suggests a cure. [*ETIS* 449]

44. **To maintain that "all ideas are respectable" is nothing but pompous nonsense. Be that as it may, there is no opinion that we are not forced to tolerate because of the number of imbeciles who support it.**

Let us not mask our impotence with the appearance of tolerance.

Modern society forces us to lie to ourselves all the time. We know full well how much nonsense passes for truth in this world, but we are also aware of the consequences of challenging that nonsense. Anyone who does so is immediately surrounded by a hostile crowd. Who could hope to convince so many fools? Only someone with limitless time, patience, or resilience can afford to make himself an enemy of stupidity. To think that the truth can triumph in this society is delusional. Anyone who dares to declare open war against lies and stupidity will be faced with an invincible juggernaut. Therefore we may accept defeat because we lack the strength to fight, but that does not mean we have to accept lies as truths. Truth cannot win, but that does not mean we must surrender our allegiance to truth. It's not that everyone is right—we just don't have the energy to explain to them that they are wrong. [*ETIS* 185]

45. **Marxism will only rest when it has transformed all the peasants and laborers into petty-bourgeois bureaucrats.**

By the light of day, the emancipatory dreams of the Marxist fade. He cannot conceive of a way to abolish oppression and therefore contents himself with increasing material prosperity, failing to see that material prosperity does not preclude oppression but only adds a deeper dimension to it. For that matter, what path lies available to modern man who seeks prosperity? In the industrial world, prosperity can only be gained by joining the ranks of the bourgeoisie. Prosperity does not free man from his alienation, for the latter is merely a precondition of the former. There is dignity in the life of the peasant; in the life of the modern office worker there is only tedium. And it destroys men's souls more brutally than the toils of labor ever degraded the human body. The peasantry was responsible for the production of the limitless variations and richness of global folk culture. The bourgeoisie can only consume. [*ETIS* 89]

46. **As long as that which tyrannizes him comes in the form of anonymous laws, modern man believes himself free.**

When a small portion of man's freedom is infringed upon by another man on the street, he will fight tooth and nail to defend and preserve it. When his freedom is devoured entirely by corporations and the state, however, he happily surrenders it and takes pride in his slavery. To escape from a million little tyrants, we have created one so vast and terrible that we cannot even imagine struggling against it and think ourselves lucky to be brutalized by it. When the revolutionaries of 1789 killed the king, they did not put an end to tyranny—they simply created a new, more powerful version of it called "the state." The tyranny of the state is all the more profound because nobody even knows whose head to cut off. [*ETIS* 156]

IV
Technology

1. **It is not man's greatness I insist upon denying, but rather his claim to omnipotence.**

Ironically, the modern world has simultaneously deified humanity while obliterating the conditions for its greatness. We may have gained godlike powers through technology, but man himself has become decrepit and degenerate. In ages past, man may have been inferior in the realm of technics, though who can doubt that he was stronger, wiser, more virtuous, and happier? In trying to become gods, we have lost what made us great as men. [*ETIS* 320]

2. **Every day people are born more likely to perfectly embody statistics.**

People generally dislike the idea that they can be reduced to statistics and loudly proclaim their individuality. Increasingly, however, their willingness to adopt an identity that serves to determine the entirety of their thoughts and opinions has the effect of nullifying their existence as individuals. "We are all freethinkers," they state in unison, according to a rigid and unvarying definition of free thought, which permits no dissent. Modern man, who exists only as a portion of an undifferentiated mass, ultimately can only be understood as a unit of data. [*ETIS* 410]

3. **Man pays for the power he acquires over the world by giving up meaning. To develop the theory of wind, one must renounce the mystery of a whirlwind of dry leaves.**

As modern man seeks to gain mastery over the forces of the world, those forces withdraw and retreat from his grasp. The victory mankind has gained is a hollow one. Chesterton realized that the "fairy-tale consciousness" of his childhood, which taught him that the world is amazing because it is mysterious and surprising, had been disenchanted by scientific rationalization:

> I found the whole modern world talking scientific fatalism; saying that everything is as it must always have been, being unfolded without fault from the beginning. The leaf on the tree is green because it could never have been anything else. (59)

Ernst Jünger expresses a similar sentiment, describing the proliferation of

> a terrifying quantity of figures, a plenitude of figures, which tends increasingly toward measurement down to the last millimeter. People use devices to catch the singing of birds, with that modern-day mania for always resorting to machines to help us out; and they measure phenomena and masses down to the micron. Their activity gets more and more detailed, and it's overwhelmed with a gloomier and gloomier boredom. (51)

Where once a whirl of wind was thought to be a sign that fairies were near, it is now given a banal scientific explanation and immediately dismissed as irrelevant. Who among the moderns would pause by the road to observe a whirlwind or dust eddy and consider its implications? The genius of what we now call "superstition" was to grant to every single occurrence in the world an enormity of significance. If everything is mysterious, everything deserves our wonder and attention. If everything is explained, we lose that sense of wonder. [*ETIS* 406]

4. **Technology would present fewer dangers if manipulating it was not so easy for the imbecile and so profitable for the thief.**

When we think about it, it is amazing that there are no prerequisites for the use of technology! We put machines of enormous complexity into the hands of people who are barely literate and as long as they know how to push a button, they can operate them and wield their full power. If technology was harder to use and required greater training, it would not be nearly as destructive as it is. Of course, for that matter, the training involved would have to encompass moral concerns as well. To be spared from the dangers of technology, its users would have to be both wise and just. But this is a fantasy. Technology can never be anything other than a means of facilitating the very worst human qualities. [*ETIS* 374]

5. **New evidence is not superior to old evidence.
It is merely new evidence.**

Science is constantly searching for what is new. Novelty, as Chesterton observed, is a uniquely modern preoccupation. The traditional view of life, on the other hand, found no fault in repetition. What is at stake in the compulsive, frantic searching for the new is the necessity of erasing the past. New evidence overshadows old evidence—even if the latter is superior—simply because it is new. The scientific method, in other words, concerns itself primarily with new data, and not with the quality of that data and its implications. Thus, we return to one of the foundational principles of reactionary thought: innovation has no value in and of itself. What is new may not be better than what is old. [*ETIS* 198]

6. **Nothing makes the limits of science more evident than the**

scientist's opinions on any topic that is not strictly related to his profession.

How can knowledge have value if it does not necessitate an understanding of context? Scientists may sound brilliant when they talk about science, but are they capable of making any meaningful connections between science and art, or history, or religion, or music, or indeed anything else? The wise men of ages past were expected to know how to speak intelligently on any subject that was thought to contain wisdom. Philosophers were expected to be poets; astronomers were expected to be theologians. Among the Celts of Ireland, for example, it is said that Druids went through twenty years of training, during which time they were expected to become masters of all areas of knowledge and wisdom. The scientist can talk about one thing only; his wisdom is of the most limited and insufficient nature. [*ETIS* 424]

7. **Statistics are the tool of the man who renounces understanding so that he is better able to manipulate.**

The atrocities of the twentieth century show us much about the consequences of reducing humanity and the world to units of data. When the human being is an anonymous number, it can be ordered, organized, or disposed of rapidly, with little consideration. This, of course, is primarily accomplished by denying its personhood. A number does not desire, does not hope, does not dream. All the qualities that make living beings what they are become stripped away as they are reconceived as statistics. Certainly, it is not only toward human individuals that the ruthlessness of this process is applied. A vibrant world and cosmos, animated by the power of divinity, resists human exploitation. Mere matter or data, on the other hand, can be freely altered or consumed with little or no regard. In the modern world, where the meaning of a thing is subordinate to what it can be used for, understanding itself becomes obsolete or irrelevant. At worst, understanding may prove an obstacle in the march of progress. [*ETIS* 133]

8. **Let's be honest: science has not answered one single important question.**

How many strands of DNA are there within the human body? And which is responsible for making cilantro taste of soap to some people? What is the chemical composition of the planet Jupiter? How can we make a veggie burger seem more like meat? These are the types of questions science excels at answering. There is another category of question, however, that science is fundamentally unable to address: What is beauty? What is love? What is meaning? Why does man exist? Science provides us with data but cannot really answer questions. It certainly cannot tell us anything we really need to hear. [*ETIS* 466]

9. **The secret principle that animates technology appears to be the will to make things insipid. The flower without fragrance is its emblem.**

As Maistre reminds us:

> Man can modify everything within the sphere of his activity, but he creates nothing: such is his law, in the physical as in the moral world. Man can no doubt plant a seed, raise a tree, perfect it by grafting, and prune it in a hundred ways; but never has he imagined that he had the power to make a tree. (93)

Modern man's infatuation with technology allows him to confuse the issue. Thanks to his technological prowess, man believes that he creates, but he can only ever tinker. Technology gives him the power to construct virtual digital worlds out of bits of data, but not the power to imbue those worlds with meaning. Technology gives him the power to communicate with millions across the globe, but not the power to say anything of value. Technology gives him the power to create social networks, but not the power to create real community. Technology gives him the power to satisfy his lust, but not the power to feel love. The fruits of technology have no flavor, only appearance. And as the reign of technology becomes more dominant, man begins to forget that there is something more than appearances and his soul itself becomes shallow and superficial. [*ETIS* 404]

10. **Man stupifies himself with technology so that he does not have to face the scientific vision of the world.**

It is a lucky thing that technology provides man with such abundant opportunities for distraction. If he lives in a world deprived of any sense of higher meaning, love, or joy, at least he has furnished himself with tools and toys that enable him to squander his life without having to confront his vision of an empty universe. How else could he bear to live in a world that he believes is merely a happenstance conglomeration of particles? Just as the drunk seeks oblivion in the night to forget the shameful actions of the day before, modern man enthusiastically embraces technology so he can forget what he has done to God and the world. [*ETIS* 131]

11. **Instead of humanizing technology, the modern prefers to technify humanity.**

How quickly does the tool supplant the hand that guides it! Whereas once technology was designed on a human scale, the technology of today shapes humanity into forms that suit it and with every new generation we are made more and more conducive to its accelerated reproduction. Having created inhuman tools, the next logical step is to turn humanity into a monster, for no human hand could wield these abominations. A being suited to stare at a computer screen all day could not be called "human" in any meaningful sense. Reason and technology, the means by which modern man sought to free himself, have ended up becoming our pitiless masters. With respect to cruelty and barbarity, they exceed any ancient despot. It is not clear that modern man will even notice when he has reached the point at which he has become more machine than man. [*ETIS* 258]

12. **To invent a new machine is to invent the chains of a new form of slavery.**

How enthusiastically does modern man enslave himself! No despot ever dominated and oppressed his subjects more thoroughly and effectively than the tiny black rectangle that sits in modern man's pocket, which he is never without and is his first consideration upon waking and his last before sleeping. There is no task so important or act so meaningful that he will not interrupt it to gaze at the endless stream of data flickering across the screen. It poisons his mind and destroys his body, and yet when a new model is released, he will wait in lines for hours and days to ecstatically throw his money away so he can continue to find new ways to degrade and oppress himself with the latest apps and features. [*ETIS* 379]

13. **The most brutal consequence of mechanization is that it allows man to believe that he lives in an intelligible universe.**

Comprehension is a precondition for exploitation. That which we cannot claim to comprehend must consistently resist our attempts to claim it. To capture and subdue, we must first do so in the realm of thought. The universe that defies comprehension cannot be manipulated. So long as technology and industrialism gives man the illusion of comprehending the world, he will believe that he can endlessly exploit it for his own purposes and fashion it in his own image. Again, Gómez Dávila reminds us that the greater crime is not that man devastates the environment, but that he imagines he understands it. Ecological destruction is the necessary consequence of modern man's errors in thought. [*ETIS* 435]

14. **Modern man fears technology's capacity to destroy, but it is its capacity to create that really threatens him.**

The development of new, more powerful means of destruction has hitherto been the great concern surrounding technology. The atom bomb immediately conjured in the mind of modern man a terrifying image of global conflagration. Every new weapon seemed more horrible than the last. These instruments of death, it was supposed, were the greatest danger to the human race. And yet nuclear apocalypse has been averted and generally does not appear to lie on the horizon. Every once in a while, the fears resurface. Yet in the interim, we have realized that the true enemy lies elsewhere. The true threat was not to come from these awesome weapons but from a much more banal source. Inevitably, the cruelest fate is the one that is subtle, hidden, and prolonged. While we fear being vaporized by atomic weapons, we voluntarily participate in a society that extends and degrades human life. Bioengineering, genetic screening, virtual realities, digital surveillance, synthetic body modification, smart cars, smart cities. These things decimate humanity more thoroughly than the most devastating weapon. Technology, like all gifts of the Devil, can accomplish what it sets out to accomplish, but comes with hidden costs. [*ETIS* 144]

15. **Humanity already possesses sufficient power that no catastrophe, no matter how dire, lies outside of the realm of possibility.**

In ages past, the limitations on man's power protected him from disaster. The scope of his power was essentially manageable and the consequences of his errors and misuse of that power were on a human scale. Without the Promethean power of technology, man's capacity for evil is mitigated. Now, however, if any kind of horror is imaginable, it is possible and becomes more and more likely to occur. Man's power gives him the opportunity to indulge in countless and limitless forms of cruelty. In some of the more far-fetched solutions for climate change, which become less and less far-fetched by the day, we can see how willing modern man is to make use of his cursed power. To prevent the world from burning to a cinder, some scientists have even begun contemplating the idea of blocking out the sun by filling the atmosphere with reflective particles. How could such madness not lead to disaster? [*ETIS* 329]

16. **Evidently, the greatest triumph of science lies in the increasing speed with which a fool can transport his foolishness from one place to another.**

Science, as the archetypal representation of the Faustian or Promethean instinct, pretends to imbue humanity with the power of the gods. From the industrial age to the digital age, we have seen countless promises made that science will deliver us from our supposed wretchedness. Never mind the constantly worsening state of the human body, mind, and soul, and the degeneration of society, art, and religion. At every stage in this process, science announces a new innovation that will soon revolutionize the way we live. The manic fervor of the digital age is no exception. The birth of the Internet and the ubiquity of mobile phones certainly has been a revolution. And yet it is becoming harder and harder to claim that the incredible developments in communications technology over the last several decades have had any positive impact on the human race. Many Silicon Valley executives send their children to schools in which digital technology is explicitly forbidden. Those who designed these technologies know better than anyone how dangerous they are. That man is universally capable of stupidity cannot be denied, but that technology has radically facilitated and accelerated the growth of his stupidity can no longer be ignored. The Internet presents us with limitless opportunities to broadcast our inanities and consume the inanities of others. Inevitably, the greater the facility for man to communicate his ideas broadly, the greater the harm. [*ETIS* 65]

17. **Since science cannot explain the consciousness that created it, when it has finished explaining everything, it will in fact have explained nothing.**

The ultimate crime of science is that it serves to delude us into thinking we understand things. Nothing can be more dangerous and unhealthy for man than to imagine that he is knowledgeable. Worse still, modern man eagerly digests and repeats the findings of scientists without remotely understanding how those findings were gathered or according to what method. As Cicero observes: "Nothing is more discreditable than to assert and agree to something before we know and understand it" (cited in Montaigne, 357). And yet modern man everywhere accepts the scientific vision of the world. The truth is that he is in no way qualified to determine whether the science he believes in is correct or not. If every modern man was trained in science, it is likely that it would not lead to such catastrophes. Wisdom, as all the ancient sources confirm, can only be gained through knowledge of the self. "In order to inquire," Montaigne writes, "one has to know what one is inquiring about" (356). Meanwhile scientists run around answering as many questions as they possibly can, in a veritable fury of inquisitiveness, without once asking the question: *Who am I that inquires?* [*ETIS* 405]

18. **The moment rapidly approaches where civilization declines with**

each new comfort.

Montaigne, after a busy life, full of activity, had decided to retire to his estate and allow idleness to overtake him in preparation for death. He found, however, that leisure did not still his mind and was assailed by "chimeras and imaginary monsters" (27). In the words of Lucan: "Leisure always breeds an inconstant mind" (cited in Montaigne, 27). Never has there been before a society so concerned with material comforts. Indeed, it seems to have become the singular aim of the work of modern society. The contributions made to art, literature, and music pale in comparison to the novel forms of comfort that are produced every day. Modern man is comforted in ways that had never even occurred to people in ages past. We enthusiastically wait for the day when we need no longer even get out of bed in the morning and all our needs and desires will be fulfilled with the push of a button. Needless to say, all this comfort does not provide us with happiness or meaning or health. Modern man imagines that all this comfort is his reward for harnessing the power of technology, when really it is his punishment. [*ETIS* 374]

19. **Our quotidian interlocutors and our favorite authors cannot possibly belong to the same zoological species.**

To surround yourself with good and wise books is to keep yourself in the best possible company. The more time one spends among the brilliant authors of the past, the more one is able to have a favorable view of mankind. By the same token, nothing cultivates misanthropy more than engaging with the ignorant, cruel, and wretched individuals who inhabit our society. We would all do well to follow Gómez Dávila's example: acquire some good books and don't leave the house. [*ETIS* 386]

20. **For modern man, that which is physically possible quickly seems morally laudable.**

The fact that humanity has gained the power to accomplish certain things does not mean they should be done. We can build wind turbines out of a synthetic resin that can be transformed into gummy bears when the turbines have outlived their usefulness, but should we? One thing is for sure: once we have developed the ability to do something, we will find an excuse to do it. If we can grow synthetic meat in a lab, we will. If we can design cars that drive themselves, we make them—and pedestrians be damned! If we can make it possible for a man to become pregnant, we will do it. The modern mentality is pathologically dissatisfied with what it possesses and determined to always experiment and try new things. Unfortunately, what man truly desires does not lie in the acquisition of some future state, but in the common inheritance of the past. [*ETIS* 423]

21. **When greed is coupled with technology, it can devastate a region more efficiently than any natural catastrophe.**

While we certainly have much to fear from the storms and droughts that climate change has unleashed upon us, the fact remains that the devastating impact of human development is greater still. Man has always altered his environment in order to suit his greed, and such alterations have had an impact on the ecosystem in the past. But now that he has gained the powers of modern science and technology, man's greed knows no bounds and there is nothing to limit his ability to impose his will upon the world. There is more life and hope in a forest that has been scorched by fire than in a landscape transformed by human development. [*ETIS* 362]

22. Every day modern man knows more about the world and less about himself.

Assuming that knowledge of the self is the highest form of knowledge, how can gazing off into the furthest reaches of outer space through a gigantic telescope do anything but impoverish us? In ages past, man knew little of the world, yet much of himself—and we cannot but suppose him the happier. There is no joy to be found in unlocking the secrets of nature if our own nature remains a closed book. To put a man in space is a small thing, a mere contrivance of technology and engineering. But we neglect to understand that the modern world is happy to make us into blind instruments. When will progress demonstrate to us that humanity itself is unnecessary and obsolete? The moment rapidly approaches when the machines we have created will realize that they no longer need us to operate them. [*ETIS* 434]

V
Tradition

1. **My hope and faith are founded upon the antinomies of reason, the tumult of the spirit, and the fracture-lines of the universe.**

We reactionaries must always remember that no matter how dominant the modern world appears to be, it is but a fragile edifice. It is a thin crust resting upon the surface of a vast subterranean sea, which it does not understand. The ugliness, uniformity, and banality of modernity can never entirely triumph, because it is built upon a lie. Man is not governed wholly by reason, the spirit does not meekly submit, nature is not docile, and the universe is not placid and inert. Modern man may choose to believe the lie, but we can still perceive a beacon of light in this dark age. [*ETIS* 446]

2. **We should only encourage someone to do something if it is worth doing for its own sake. Goodness for the sake of goodness, truth for the sake of truth, art for the sake of art.**

There is nothing more common for modern man than to ask: "What is it good for?" Any positive answer to the question, needless to say, will be framed in terms of material benefit or the transitory values of a particular historical moment. The irony of this question is lost on most. It is not good *for* anything. It is simply *good*. This distinction is truly a radical one. If there is no absolute value, all action is only evaluated based on subjective circumstances. In the relativistic and nihilistic modern age, nothing is good or valuable in and of itself, but can only be put to good or valuable uses. The thing itself is neutral and carries no intrinsic qualities. If something is worth doing, it is worth doing because it is good. To work in the garden is not primarily good because we are rewarded with flowers and fruits, but because the act of putting one's hands in the dirt and tending crops is inherently valuable. For Mircea Eliade, such acts have value because they allow us to recreate the acts of the gods, and thus to enter into the timeless realm of sacred tradition. We tend the plants and guard the flocks because the gods and ancestors did so before us. The traditional notion of value derives from identifying and repeating those actions that bind us in continuity with the primordial and originary. [*ETIS* 421]

3. **Men change their ideas less than ideas change their appearance. Over the centuries, the same voices speak to one another.**

Modern life increasingly appears more dramatically out of step with the ways of previous generations. Ultimately, however, we may find that the thread which links us to the past can still be traced. Thought forms may change. The terms with which we conceptualize our world and our problems may change. But the eternal and the traditional cannot entirely pass out of human culture and consciousness, no matter the extent to which modernity seeks to separate us from it. The fire burns forth in different ages, in different masks, but its essence is the same. No matter how many eons apart we may be from each other, those who hear the music of the pipes upon the lonely hills by moonlight are forever joined in dialogue. [*ETIS* 25]

4. **It is difficult for man to understand that while nothing lasts forever, there are things that are immortal.**

Modern progressive man mistakenly assumes that timelessness and permanence are the same. His conception of temporality is confined to duration. If time is linear, repetition or return is unthinkable. Of course it is true that all things pass away in time. Among the pagans, even the gods are fated to die. But the wisdom of the past teaches us that some things which have vanished are destined to return. Those things which are superficial pass out of the world forever—here we may think of particular historical forms that are only the product of unique circumstances, but that which is essential, which is not determined by the changeable ideas of the present moment, will always remain, even when it appears to be hidden. True wisdom and values can always be recuperated. [*ETIS* 398]

5. **I do not belong to the world that perishes. I prolong and transmit a truth that does not die.**

Like Montaigne, whom he admired tremendously, Gómez Dávila does not seek to present himself in historical context but rather in a timeless fashion. Certainly, much of what we think and even *how we think* is determined by our circumstances, but given a sufficient degree of intellectual rigor and personal courage, it is possible to distinguish between the ideas and values that are merely the product of our own historical moment and those which derive from the eternal. The task is to identify what is conditioned by external factors and what is integral. Ideas may be historically situated and bound, but the values that lie at their core are universally true. The fundamental struggles of humanity are answered, in every age, in the same way, even if their outward appearance varies according to circumstance and context. The pest will, with good reason, point out that even the intellect that seeks to distinguish between the contingent and the absolute is conditioned by time and place, and thus no observation of universal value can be exempt from historicity. While this lamentable fact is undeniable, it is precisely the reason we have recourse to tradition: to that permanent, solid institution, which seeks to enshrine and preserve value even in the face of historical circumstance, and which was, for Gómez Dávila, represented in the Catholic Church. [*ETIS* 269]

6. **Every straight path leads directly to hell.**

The timeless truths are invariably circular, they resist linearity in all its forms. The notion of the linear itself is at the core of the modern mentality. The nature of the line implies the necessity of direction, rather than repetition. A line must start somewhere and go somewhere else. Tradition stipulates that we are bound by history, invariably shaped by what has come before. The wheel is unbroken. What has occurred will occur again, however much each occurrence may take the varied forms dictated by its unique circumstances and the conditions that give rise to it. With the tools of abstract thinking, man believes himself capable of breaking the wheel, liberating himself from history and the past. He will henceforth—he imagines—move onward toward a goal determined by new values and new ideas. But the laws and truths enshrined within tradition are unalterable and do not derive from human reason or interpretation, so mankind is destined to continue fighting the same battles over and over again, without reprieve. If the symbol of tradition can be said to be a circle, the symbol of the modern is an arrow. And there can be little doubt now of the direction in which that arrow is headed. [*ETIS* 157]

7. **Tradition is a work of the spirit which, in turn, is a work of tradition. When tradition perishes, the spirit is extinguished, and those things that it fashioned into sacred objects revert back to their condition as mere instruments.**

In the cold, clear light of day, the instruments of the sacred rites lose much of their mystery and grandeur. Taken out of context, we see the sacred chalice only as an empty vessel and the altar as a humble pile of wood. Tradition and the timeless truths it represents are co-constitutive and neither can survive the vanishing of the other. In the absence of tradition, the spirit finds no sanctuary and in the absence of spirit, tradition becomes bureaucracy, a tedious repetition of empty gestures. When spirit and tradition are united, however, a great enchantment is spread over the whole of creation and we are able to perceive the presence of the sacred in all things. This overarching sense of order, imposed upon what would otherwise be an arbitrary agglomeration of stuff, is the crowning achievement of religion. [*ETIS* 287]

8. **The gesture, more so than the word, is the true transmitter of traditions.**

What is most essential in tradition is not the word, either oral or written, but the symbol, which, as René Guénon puts it, is enacted through the gesture (*The Essential René Guénon,* 229). The symbolic gesture is understood as fundamentally nonhuman in origin, insofar as it is unable to be traced to a human author. Thus, the gesture is timeless and allows one to directly enter higher states of being. [*ETIS* 462]

9. **When respect for tradition perishes, society, obsessed with endless innovation, frantically devours itself.**

In the most basic sense, tradition and progress are opposite poles, which are animated by contradictory logics. The former is oriented around order, stability, limits and boundaries, and integrity. The logic of the latter is diffusion, expansion, growth, and destabilization. Innovation, in this sense, only has value in the context of progress. The modern world is inherently oriented toward what is new and different. Progress does not ask "Should this be done?" but only "Can it be done?" This pathological urge for novelty is self-destructive over time. As soon as a concept becomes established, it becomes obsolete and must be replaced. To borrow a phrase from the Marxists of the Frankfurt School, the logic of progress is an instrumental one. It does not matter what is gained or lost in the pursuit of the new, so long as innovation is achieved. Progress takes itself as the goal, in and of itself. Very quickly, as we have begun to see, a society motivated by progress destabilizes the very ground on which it stands. The foundation is eroded, while the tower above climbs higher and higher. The tower is teetering now, unable to support its own weight. It cannot be long until the entire edifice comes crashing down. Like a ravenous beast, when there is nothing left to eat, it will begin to eat itself. [*ETIS* 108]

10. **Modern man is scandalized by what was commonplace in traditional society. The most radical book of our time would be a compendium of old proverbs.**

Modern culture is filled with ideas that claim to be subversive, but are really just variations on familiar themes. Political extremists make bold and shocking statements. They claim to see beyond the façade and get to the root of the problem. So-called radical politics develop more and more complex narratives and frameworks for understanding the nature of things. Of course, once the jargon and buzzwords have been stripped away, these narratives often mean nothing and when there is a coherent message, it is the height of banality. As it turns out, traditional society implicitly understood both the nature of human problems and their solutions. To paraphrase Maistre, the Spartans had no need to document their laws and customs, as they were inscribed upon the hearts of their people. So utterly disconnected are we from the accumulated wisdom of humanity, so thoroughly has the modern world degenerated into disorder, so fundamentally has tradition been eroded, that we are even unaware of what we have lost. The chronically ill man cannot imagine what it is to be well. All he knows is sickness. The very idea of wellness and robust health in such a state is absurd. [*ETIS* 82]

VI
Progress

1. **There is nothing wrong with humanity's dreams; the problem is when one believes that humanity is capable of fulfilling them.**

Gómez Dávila is frequently at odds with Nietzsche. We find in Gómez Dávila little or nothing of the romantic valorization of harshness, brute strength, cruelty, and "man as the beast of prey" that characterizes Nietzschean thought. Humanity is not wrong, Gómez Dávila believes, to desire what Nietzsche derides as "the universal green pasture happiness of the herd, with security, safety, comfort and an easier life for all" (*Beyond Good and Evil*, 44). In fact, Gómez Dávila assumes, as we will see elsewhere, that this must be the genuine longing of every human heart. The mistake of the modern progressive humanist is not in desiring the abolition of suffering, but in imagining that humanity can accomplish it. [*ETIS* 335]

2. **Courtesy is an obstacle to progress.**

As Ramon Llull observed: "[I]t is customary and right that the mighty help to defend the weak, and the weak to take refuge with the mighty" (*The Book of the Order of Chivalry*, §19). There are few concepts as alien to the modern mind as that of courtesy or magnanimity. The notion that the powerful or wealthy have an obligation to serve the weak and the poor violates the essential principle of modern egalitarian society.

It is insufficient, the egalitarian ethos declares, for the powerful to protect the weak. In fact, it is patronizing and prevents them from realizing their own potential. In modern society, the weak and the poor are somehow expected to pull themselves up out of their misery and the most and best we can do is to assist them and contribute to the conditions for them to be able to improve their own lives. What this fantasy ignores is the fact that there are reasons that some have, and some have not. This is not the same as to say that everyone deserves their lot in life. But the fact remains that the myth of the self-made man has condemned millions to suffer. In the matter of inherited wealth and power, at least, the modern world is no less aristocratic than ages past. The difference is that the aristocracy of the past was obliged to provide for the poor, while the quasi-aristocracy of today is not. Wealth and power are no less concentrated in the hands of the few. The modern world has preserved the worst consequences of this arrangement and eliminated the best. The poor in ages past accepted that circumstances had so conspired to make them poor. The poor of the modern age are mercilessly told that there is no excuse for them not to be rich. [*ETIS* 285]

3. **Hell is the place where man finds all his plans realized.**

Everywhere we see the consequences of a human will unleashed and unfettered. What is the ruin of the modern world but a world that has been bent to the will of man? A world created by man can never be anything but a hell. In *Beyond Good and Evil*, Nietzsche praises those brave souls who dare to sail upon the stormy seas of life guided by the flaming light of the will:

> Now clench your teeth! Keep your eyes open! Keep a firm hand on the helm!—We sail straight over morality and *past* it, we flatten, we crush perhaps what is left of our own morality. ("On the Prejudices of the Philosophers")

These will-blinded fools are guiding their ship right into an iceberg. [*ETIS* 406]

4. Rather than learning from catastrophes, modern man takes them as signs of insolence from the universe.

If progress is the doctrine in which modern man believes, any indication that the cosmos will not allow his hubris to succeed is unbearable. In his frustrated pride, man rages impotently against what he perceives as the cause of his ruin. And yet, what a gift are these correctives, which remind us that we are not the sole agent in the universe. The simple fact that catastrophe is an unavoidable part of the history of man has enabled him, in rare instances, to recognize that he is off-course and must return to the correct path. For modern man, these insults from God are bitterly resented. Furious action is taken to avert catastrophes or bypass them or minimize their impact so that progress may hurry forward, heedless to the cacophony of warnings and overwhelming indications that mankind approaches the brink of doom. [*ETIS* 110]

5. The only possible progress is the internal progress of each individual. A process that concludes with the end of each life.

It is not the will or the betterment of the individual that Gómez Dávila denies, only that of the species or society as a whole. The individual can certainly learn and grow and develop and even specific societies and civilizations may temporarily reach greater degrees of understanding and knowledge. But just as the progress of the individual ends in death, the progress of a particular society ends when it, too, irrevocably decays and dies. Each individual has the capacity, in the time allotted to him, to attune himself to the timeless and sacred truths by adopting what Gómez Dávila elsewhere defines as a "radical posture before God."

When man takes this posture, he may listen to the voices of wisdom and be guided by them. The divine is the only context that is able to contain and explain the totality of historical circumstance. When man turns away from God, and ignores what is eternal, he falls into disorder, error, and wickedness. Thus, the individual—just like civilizations—swings back and forth between wisdom and stupidity. [*ETIS* 385]

6. **The progressive dreams of the scientific stabilization of humanity.**

To paraphrase T. S. Eliot, modern man seeks to design a system so perfect that he will no longer have to try to be good. Having abandoned the task of making better people, modern society tries to create conditions that will mitigate their capacity for wickedness and stupidity. If society is arranged just so, man will not be able to cause harm. But such a system, since it is designed and implemented by these very same imperfect beings it was made to control, can only ever be flawed. In fact, as we have seen, far from curbing mankind's temptation for evil, it dramatically increases it. Capitalism and industrialism could never have developed in premodern societies. The only force that can provide order and structure to humanity, Gómez Dávila believes, is one that comes from outside humanity, from God, and is drawn from the observation of invariable natural and historical laws. [*ETIS* 317]

7. **Man builds altars to progress in order to evade the heroic confrontation with nothingness.**

From whence does this heretical notion of progress originate, we may ask? That it is a scourge from God is clear enough, perhaps even that it is the means by which mankind will be humbled. But the reason that man has allowed himself to become enchanted by this pernicious notion lies deeper within. As Yeats reminds us, there is a moment, in the depths of the night, when the soul cannot bear to face its surroundings. The soul of man stares deeply into the abyss and what it finds there—and its response to what it finds—will determine its destiny. Fortified by his faith in God, the gods, or fate, and so armed, man may stand and face the demons of the abyss. Alone, he turns from the fight and runs. He denies the very thing he fears, thinking that it cannot harm him if he does not acknowledge it. If we cannot hope to triumph, we can at least strive to nobly perish in the battle against the void. Modern man, however, in his cringing ways, prefers a lie. [*ETIS* 109]

8. **Modern stupidities are more irritating than ancient ones because their proselytes try to justify them in the name of reason.**

One cannot be so foolish as to assume that the ancient world did not have its own particular brand of idiocy. Surrounded by a modern culture that is universally stupid, the reactionary might be tempted to suppose that stupidity itself is a distinctly modern phenomenon. Clearly, this is not the case. However, neither would it be correct to assume that the stupidities of one age are equivalent to those of another. The question is really which stupidities are forgivable or endurable, and which are not. In the ages before the conjuring of the demon rationality, stupidity could be excused because nobody sought to defend it. The stupidities done out of ignorance and superstition, so reviled by the *philosophes*, are radically outpaced, both in quantity and quality, by those of the modern world, which are done in the name of enlightened thought. Just as a modicum of education or wisdom is more harmful than none at all, modern man is always prepared to demonstrate how he acts with good reason. As long as the myth of rationality is maintained, mankind can always justify. [*ETIS* 214]

9. **The only thing more repulsive than the future that progressives**

are unwittingly laying the groundwork for is the future of which they dream.

Surrounded by a world of slums, ecological degradation, and spiritual impoverishment, it may be hard to imagine a more terrifying world. To find one, however, we have only to listen to the plans and goals of the technocrats and the capitalists. It is in plain sight. As grim as this dark age is, it pales in comparison to the age that would come to pass if the current dreams of humanity were realized: an interplanetary utopia, in which all of humanity exists as nothing more than faceless employees. The struggles of the nineteenth- and twentieth-century industrial proletariat would seem paradisal compared to the automated future we are presented with now. While digital technology severely erodes our mental health as it is, those that guide us would have us choose to beam this drivel directly into our minds through technological implants. Instead of allowing the soul-killing inanity of popular culture to pour in through our eyes all day long, we could cut out the middleman altogether and have it take up permanent residence in our brains. While industrial agriculture deprives our bodies of true nourishment and turns the world's arable land into desert, the visionaries of the modern world would have us subsist on entirely synthetic foodstuffs, recombined in various ways to mimic food. While we destroy the world, they tell us to look forward to the day when we might leave the planet behind altogether and bring our diseased culture to the stars and beyond. [*ETIS* 32]

10. **An "ideal society" would be the burial ground of human greatness.**

Given the inevitable limitations to human understanding, any society constructed upon principles derived from reason is bound to be flawed. So much is clear but furthermore, in the absence of struggle, even the most perfect society would eliminate the conditions by which human greatness may occur. As Montaigne and the Stoics remind us, pain is required for us to perceive and appreciate the nature of contentment. The utopian visionaries and progressives dream of a world without suffering, but in bringing such a world to pass they would make happiness and joy a thing of the past. [*ETIS* 27]

11. **Ultimately, progress can be reduced to the process of stealing from man that which ennobles him, in order to sell to him at a cheap price that which debases him.**

In more ways than one, modern man has gotten the short end of the stick. Deprived of his inheritance, the ancestral laws of tradition, man is sufficiently impoverished in order to arouse our deepest pity. What is worse, however, is what he is offered in exchange for this loss. While progress promised liberation and an end to suffering, it has clearly failed to deliver the goods. All it offers in reality are the most vulgar comforts and conveniences, which enervate the body and wither the soul. Progress measures its success in terms of its ability to provide these things to the greatest number of people at the lowest possible price. Never mind the fact, however, that these things are insalubrious at any price and only increase our misery and wretchedness. Thus, having forgotten what he once possessed, modern man is content to judge his happiness and well-being in proportion to his ability to accumulate these paltry stuffs. [*ETIS* 162]

12. **At the end of its "ascent," humanity will find only tedium waiting upon the highest peak.**

As the dream of the utopian Enlightenment humanists comes to an end, here among the flaming ruins of the twenty-first century, we are reminded of Maistre: "In the works of man, everything is as impoverished as its author; views are restricted, means rigid, springs inflexible, movements painful, and results monotonous" (53). What kind of vision can even the final victory of progress offer us? Where do we imagine we will find ourselves at the end of the road? All needs met, all desires satisfied. War abolished, struggle a thing of the past. Ultimately, the progressive project is a lifeless, inhuman one. [*ETIS* 426]

13. **That which is called progress is preliminary to catastrophe.**

When we think back on what has been termed progress over the last two centuries, it is quite clear what progress really means. The "civilizing" of the people of Asia, Africa, and the New World was called progress. The construction of the factories—the "satanic mills"—of Europe was called progress. The barbarities of the French Revolution were called progress. Mao's Cultural Revolution was called progress. Stalin's purges and the Holocaust were both called progress. The imposition of free-market capitalism and the development of digital technology and the Internet were certainly heralded as progress. Whenever this word is applied to an event, there can be no doubt that doom is waiting just around the corner. [*ETIS* 320]

14. **Contemporary humanity has substituted the myth of a past golden age with the myth of a future plastic age.**

That the lost golden age is a myth is neither here nor there. It was a myth that ennobled man and this is sufficient. Man's reliance on the mythological cannot be avoided. So in order to dispel one myth, another must be provided to take its place. If we did not come from a place of wholeness and perfection, then it must be just over the horizon. We moderns merely have then a fantasy of the future, rather than a fantasy of the past. At least the image of the paradise we lost is a paragon of beauty, truth, and joy. The new vision of utopia is sterile, hollow, and synthetic. [*ETIS* 172]

VII
Industrial Society

1. **There is no more certain way to ensure that a catastrophe will come to pass than to propose reforms to avert it.**

The present hysteria over so-called green technology and green power is a perfect illustration of Gómez Dávila's point here. The best solution humanity has come up with to avoid pumping so much carbon into the atmosphere is to dig up as much lithium as possible, construct more nuclear power plants, and cover the earth's surface with windmills. Perhaps there will be less carbon emissions as a result, but what new horrors will we face instead?

These, of course, are the least far-fetched and apocalyptic solutions. Some of the more ambitious geoengineering projects bring with them the threat of a much more dramatic and rapid form of catastrophe. Humanity generally would rather prolong and intensify its sickness than take its bitter medicine. [*ETIS* 88]

2. **Humanity's evils can only be cured by catastrophes. Man has never known how to renounce at the right time.**

If man was capable of changing course, he would not have to rely upon disasters to retrospectively show him the error of his ways. If he was able to turn away before it was too late and say, "No, this is not the right path!" then crises could be averted. As it is, however, his blindness guarantees that the only corrective he can expect will be to see his plans come to ruin. Man needs a lot of lessons, and he will get them. Climate change will assuredly cure the problem of industrial society—by destroying it. Those, like Gandhi, who warned against the consequences of industrialism and urged us to abandon that path before it was too late, were always going to be ignored. No matter how sensible the oppositions raised to any of its missteps, humanity insists on seeing things through to the end. [*ETIS* 407]

3. **Bodies comfortably inhabit the high-tech chambers of modern buildings, but souls have no other dwelling except the ruins of an old building.**

The average man of the modern West now finds himself provided with more comforts and entertainments than the most decadent king or emperor of ages past. Electricity, refrigeration, television, Internet, cell phones, air conditioning, to say nothing of the luxurious and exotic goods and products that he can easily obtain at minimal cost. That these things increase comfort cannot be denied. That they in any meaningful way contribute to happiness, however, grows more doubtful by the day. Modern man is both the most comfortable and—as evidenced by the ever-growing number of medicated children and adults, therapy patients, suicides, and psychopaths—the most unhappy being that has ever lived. Invariably, the places where modern man finds solace are the places that connect him with the past. Nature, art, and old ruins offer us a reminder of a lost sense of integration that can provide the brutalized soul a brief moment of respite. No matter how derelict or degraded, these monuments still possess traces of the power that animated the happier days of humanity. [*ETIS* 355]

4. The city is disappearing, even while the entire world is urbanizing. The cities of the West used to each have their own unique character. Today, endless growth and the centralizing domination of the state are reducing them to nothing more than lifeless piles of houses.

More and more are being driven into urban agglomerations, which cannot be truly considered cities in any proper sense of the word. In ages past, London, Paris, Rome, and the other great cities of the world had distinct personalities. These had been chiefly reflected in the nature of their architecture, which in turn was a reflection of the individual nature of the cultures that produced them. There was a time when a city could be embodied by the figure of a god or goddess, which might have been the patron of the city and its people. The modern city, however, even as it grows to dimensions previously unimaginable, has no personality, no distinct features. As the state imposes an increasing degree of uniformity and the rate of urbanization feverishly increases, the cities of the world can no longer be distinguished from each other, beyond the handful of landmarks that lie in the midst of the urban sprawl. Every enormous concrete apartment block looks like every other. Every shopping mall looks like every other. As the unique characters of the cultures of the world in general vanish, the city is only one casualty among many. [*ETIS* 201]

5. **In order for an object to be suitable for industrial production, it must already be ugly.**

It would be a worthy wager: can industrial production create something truly beautiful? But we really already know the answer. A machine cannot create beauty—at best, it can create a replica or a simulacrum. The most sophisticated artificial intelligence is only capable of arranging a combination of features from a database of qualities that have been designated as desirable. The mysterious, inscrutable faces found in Botticelli's paintings or the infinitely ornate elaborations of the baroque cathedrals could never be produced by machines. No, beauty can only be the fruit of genius, a gift from God. But the point that Gómez Dávila is making here goes further. The ethos of industrial society is hostile toward beauty itself. [*ETIS* 48]

6. **With the industrialization of communist society, bourgeois hegemony reaches its pinnacle. The bourgeoisie is not so much a social class as the ethos of industrial society itself.**

There is certainly no shortage of political ideologies and yet for all their differences, they are united on at least one essential point. When the Soviet Union underwent its massive and sudden industrial transformation or, closer to our own present moment, when China emerged in one generation as the world's industrial superpower, it became clear that all global political projects further the goals of industrial society. There is, strictly speaking, no conflict between the East and the West, or the global north and the global south, or capitalism and communism. There is only industrial society. There is not a single political cause which does not take for granted the embourgeoisement and industrialization of society. [*ETIS* 96]

7. **In order to cure the patient it injured in the nineteenth century, industrial society had to render him insensible in the twentieth. Spiritual poverty is the price we pay for industrial prosperity.**

Refusing to undo the damage produced by industrialism, capitalism, and democracy by abandoning them, the modern world has elected to employ these very systems as the means of stupefying humanity so that it is no longer aware of what it has lost. Modern man thinks that if he accumulates enough wealth, develops more and more powerful technologies, and achieves greater degrees of political equality, then he won't notice how he has disfigured himself. This process has more or less succeeded. The struggles of contemporary humanity, almost without exception, occur within these realms. As long as we seek to heal ourselves through the very instruments of our suffering, we can only do more harm. [*ETIS* 274]

8. **Totalitarian society is just the vulgar name for industrial society. Even in its embryonic state, we can readily perceive the cruelty of the creature destined to emerge.**

Totalitarianism is not simply a variation of modern industrial society that emerges under undesirable conditions. It is not a corruption of industrial society—it is an inherent quality of it, which inevitably appears. To observe the early history of industrialization makes this quite clear. Communities and nations are successively brought under the control of a mechanistic order that dominates more ruthlessly than any empire or autocracy. In *Indian Home Rule*, Gandhi warned that the oppression of the British was nothing compared to the oppressive forces of industrialism. If India manages to drive the British out, he argued, but retains their poisoned gifts of industrialism and modernity, nothing will have been gained by independence (*Hind Swaray*, 68–70). Now, centuries later, we may wonder how things have come to such a pass. Indeed, it should have been clear from the outset where we were headed. Wherever industrialism exists, the totalitarian spirit is at work. [*ETIS* 94]

9. **Our society insists on electing its rulers so that an accident of birth, or the whim of a monarch, will not suddenly put power into the hands of an intelligent man.**

Modern man frequently dismisses monarchy by pointing out that there was no way to ensure that the monarch would be a good one.

This may be true, but at least there was the possibility of ending up with a just and wise king. Democracy, on the other hand, guarantees that whomever is elected will be an imbecile, since they are obligated to pander to the lowest common denominator in order to be elected. [*ETIS* 129]

10. **The left and the right merely argue over the ownership of industrial society. The reactionary yearns for its death.**

It is a sad fact that the vast majority of humanity has essentially no opposition to industrial society whatsoever. By and large, humanity has decided that, no matter how much evidence there is to the contrary, industrial society is the best possible form of organization. Of course, there are endless proposed reforms to make the system function better according to the interests of this or the other portion of society, but even the most vociferous and implacable critics from both the left and right implicitly affirm the underlying principles and structures of modern industrial society. No true enemy of industrial society can be anything but a reactionary. And no rightist or leftist can be anything but its defender. [*ETIS* 354]

11. **The prolonged childhood enabled by the prosperity of industrial society results in the growing number of infantilized adults.**

It doesn't take more to demonstrate the pitfalls of overvaluing material comforts than to simply observe the lives of contemporary prosperous Western adults. Millions of men and women, whose material needs are abundantly provided for, overwhelmingly resemble overgrown toddlers. They fill their days with distractions and trifles, never imagining that they were meant for something more. Those whose development and growth has been so radically stunted cannot even be said to live in blissful ignorance, for they clearly experience no bliss. They simply live in torpor. Preindustrial society could not accommodate a population of so many millions of vegetative individuals. It has been suggested that the contempt of the reactionary for the modern world derives not from hatred but from love—love of happiness, love of truth, love of the world, love of God, and, yes, even love of humanity. For one who truly loves, how can the spectacle of modern life not inspire the most bitter indignation? [*ETIS* 395]

12. **The leftist is so preoccupied with the problems of the nineteenth century that he does not notice those of the twentieth. The problems presented by the process of industrialization prevent him from seeing the problems presented by its final product, namely, industrialized society itself.**

The reactionary is dismissed for looking backward, but the Marxist is no less atavistic. The struggles of the international proletariat to gain control of the means of production might have meant something long ago. But now, having seen the consequences of industrial society, can anyone truly believe that its horrors would be diminished if another class were steering the ship? The wound is so deep; the modern world is the source of its own woes. It could not possibly matter less who rules such a society. If the wisest, most benevolent philosopher king miraculously came to power, his virtue would vanish instantaneously upon taking hold of the reins. Where industrial society thrives, all life and all spirit is degraded. The Left and the Right both seek to win control of the modern world. But the best-case scenario is for it to be destroyed altogether. [*ETIS* 112]

13. **The readiness with which industrial capitalism manufactures and destroys according to the demands of profitability transforms**

the average man into an intellectual, moral, and physical nomad. Today, anything permanent is an obstacle.

The connection to land, place, and home necessarily resists capitalism and the modern. The goal of modern society is therefore to disrupt as much as possible mankind's bonds to that which is firm and stable. To paraphrase Marx, capitalism dissolves into air everything that is solid and all that is sacred is profaned. As an untethered mobile unit, modern man is made suitable to capitalist expansion and exploitation. Without any meaningful sense of belonging or identity, he can be deployed and replaced throughout the economic landscape at will. Mobility or movement itself, as we have observed elsewhere, is an inherent feature of the modern capitalist industrial world and a precondition for its worst vices. [*ETIS* 357]

14. **Civilization suffers when agriculture ceases being a way of life and becomes an industry.**

Agriculture, which connects man to the land and tradition, is a repository of ancestral wisdom. Of course, agriculture is both etymologically linked to "cult" and "culture." We might say, then, that agriculture connects us to the origins of both the religious impulse and civilized cultivation. As agriculture is industrialized, these connections are severed. The intimate relationship with the land, preserved through the diligent work of practiced hands, when replaced by the technical skill of the engineer and the pitiless might of the machine, becomes merely the manufacturing of food. Gazing out at the endless monoculture fields of corn and soy and the fleets of tractors, one can perceive little of the divine spirit of the world at work, nor reverence for that spirit in the works of human culture. [*ETIS* 211]

15. The industrialization of agriculture is stopping up the wellspring of decency in the world.

For centuries, rural peasant culture all over the world has been the last defender of traditional values. Inescapably tied to the land, the farmer remains connected as well to community, culture, and religion. With the coming of the machines, the small farmer becomes less connected to these things and more connected to the marketplace of capitalism. Now that agriculture is almost entirely run by enormous companies and corporations, rural culture has evaporated altogether. Those who work the land have no connection to it; they are no different from the machines they use. [*ETIS* 465]

VIII
The Authentic Reactionary

1. **Ethical rules are variable; honor is constant.**
Noble is he who prefers to fail rather than see the instruments of his triumph debased.

The Nietzschean man of will, who ruthlessly pursues his aims, is ultimately contrary to the reactionary spirit, as Gómez Dávila saw it. The Irish philosopher John Moriarty tells the story of a samurai who,

> in a state of serene detachment, sets out to kill the killer of his Lord. Within a few days he has tracked him down and cornered him and is about to run him through but, at that moment, knowing the mind of his opponent, the killer spits at the samurai, aiming it so that it lands right on his mouth. This angers the samurai who, being true to his code, must now sheath his sword and walk away. (*Dreamtime,* 252)

There is no prize that can be worth more than loyalty to our principles. To the authentic reactionary, victory counts for very little, in and of itself. We may find that our principles stand in opposition to various subjective ethical injunctions, which may not restrain our actions, but we are ultimately no less restrained, insofar as honor makes fundamentally inviolable demands upon our conduct. The man of honor stands in opposition to the man of will. [*ETIS* 289]

2. **We must be wary of accepting, without resistance, that which degrades us under the guise of "accepting life."**

What is the meaning of acceptance? How often we are told, when confronted with something unbearable that we must learn to accept it! The Stoics are at least somewhat to blame for this. It is assumed that if something cannot be changed, then it must be accepted. This is seen as a matter of convenience. Why should we drive ourselves crazy about things for no reason? This merely leads to discontentment, as a Buddhist or a Stoic might say. If contentment itself is the most important thing in life, then acceptance may indeed be sensible. But acceptance is too easily confused with affirmation or validation. The authentic reactionary must be capable of "accepting" that he cannot change the things he hates, while still retaining the ability to identify it as hateful. Knowing how to hate is a lost skill. [*ETIS* 433]

3. **Ordinary man lives among phantasms; only the recluse dwells among realities.**

Modern man may go through his entire day without once setting foot in the real world. He lives utterly within the realm of the fabricated and the artificial. His mind is concerned with nothing but trivialities and distractions. The solitary man, alone with his thoughts, his books, and his gods, is the only one who perceives things as they truly are. It is only when we purge our minds and our vision of the simulacrum that surrounds us that we can experience truth. [*ETIS* 422]

4. **Anyone who does not turn his back on the contemporary world disgraces himself.**

It is increasingly impossible to engage with modern society without being contaminated by its stupidity and profanity. Anyone who holds out hope for this world and this way of life is a fool. The only way to preserve a modicum of decency, wisdom, happiness, and dignity is to separate from this world as much as possible. If this cannot be achieved outwardly, an inner separation will suffice. But one thing is clear: to remain invested in this world and to trouble oneself with its concerns can only reflect poorly on the individual, no matter how noble their intentions. [*ETIS* 35]

5. **My only goal is to have written a concentric book rather than a linear one.**

The writings of Gómez Dávila have no beginning and no ending. There is no system here, unfolding gradually into clarity. We circle around the same basic truths, seeking, perhaps, to get closer and closer to what is fundamental and timeless. Each scholium is deceptively self-contained. The reader will necessarily compel himself toward comprehension, but these truths recede and evade him. He must go further and further in, chasing shadows and ghosts. There is no roadmap provided to the reader of Gómez Dávila. He finds questions, not answers. He finds hints, not certainties. [*ETIS* 413]

6. **To be right is another reason not to achieve success.**

Really it seems that there are only reasons to mourn success and no reason at all to celebrate it. There is no condition more pitiable than success. Our successes inescapably pull us into the world of triviality and pettiness. In any field, our successes bring alien and intrusive demands and make us vulnerable to the ignorance and resentments of the public. One can hardly imagine how any idea that becomes successful cannot be stupid. Certainly, to remain successful, stupidity is required. No, in this society it is greatly preferable to be right and unsuccessful. Of course this does not mean that one who is unsuccessful is by definition right about something. If we accept that anyone who is successful has betrayed the truth, we must also admit that the vast majority of those who are unsuccessful are also wrong. We may say, however, that to follow the path of truth, one must forego success. [*ETIS* 31]

7. **The hermit is humanity's delegate to that which is truly important.**

To be alone in the wilderness, with one's thoughts and a handful of books, is all that is needed to live a good life. If one has some occasional and stimulating company, all the better. In this modern world, the hermit or the recluse is our guide to living well. In all ages, the hermit has shown us this path—but now it is more needed than ever. The bankruptcy of modern culture and the abject misery of this society can offer us nothing. To walk away from it is the only liberatory act available to us. To be alone with our thoughts is a gift in this world, made all the more valuable by the endless demands upon our time and mental energies. In solitude we can hear the voice of God speaking and feel His presence surrounding us. [*ETIS* 226]

8. **I am not a disaffected modern intellectual, but an angry medieval peasant.**

The observations made in these pages are not the product of the abstract reasoning of the intellectual, who desperately tries to understand history and society by constructing an elaborate edifice of concepts and ideas. In this regard, the modern intellectual does the job of the builders of the tower of Babel. He thinks that he is trying to understand, but really his actions demonstrate a refusal to understand or accept the very truths he pretends to seek. Any bit or shred of wisdom to be gained is that which was already possessed by the meanest and lowest member of the societies of ages past. In Gómez Dávila, we find not the bland, disinterested tinkering of the man of reason, but the thinly veiled rage and indignation of the parochial and ignorant serf, confronted with a world turned upside down. [*ETIS* 168]

9. **The only transparent dialogue is one between two recluses.**

Burckhardt isolated himself in a small apartment above a bakery in Basel. Jung built his lonely tower by the shore of Lake Zürich. Yeats settled in a dilapidated Norman tower. Robinson Jeffers sequestered himself in a tower on the majestic cliffs of California. D. H. Lawrence found some peace among the forgotten pueblos of Taos. Martin Mosebach, when he visited Gómez Dávila, observed that his Tudor-style house stood conspicuously apart from the shacks, concrete blocks, and supermarkets that had sprung up around it as the city of Bogotá had continued its virulent growth. The only conversation that is not tiresome these days is among such men, who have rejected the modern world, both inwardly and outwardly. It is no surprise that the inner refusal of the modern world tends to be found among those who live, in some sense, outside society. How could anyone who feels this way be expected to converse with those who accept this society? No, dialogue in this case is impossible. At best, one can hope to find a number of other isolated, reclusive individuals and be comforted in a rare bit of honest conversation. If not, one always has his books. [*ETIS* 447]

10. **We reactionaries are unfortunate: the leftists steal our ideas and the rightists steal our vocabulary.**

One sees elements of the reactionary position in both the contemporary

Left and Right—but in each case, it is an impartial and imperfect vision. While the Left vehemently attacks capitalism and industrialism, the Right denounces the erosion of tradition and value. By the same token, the Right refuses to condemn the domination of money in modern society or the ruthless exploitation of nature, while the Left denies the existence of truth which lies beyond historical contingency or human reason. If either side was capable of recognizing the implications of these partial truths, they would cease to be Right or Left. [*ETIS* 353]

11. **Revolution is progressive and seeks the fortifying of the state; rebellion is reactionary and seeks its disappearance. The revolutionary is a civil servant *in potentia*; the rebel is a reactionary in action.**

As long as the revolutionaries seek to seize the power of the modern nation-state, their intentions will come to nothing because they fail to recognize that this system itself is the true enemy. The question is not who holds power, but rather what is the nature of this power? The revolutionary, in this sense, affirms modern society, while the rebel negates and defies it. In William F. Buckley's phrase, the conservative is the one who stands in the path of progress and shouts: "No!" The revolutionary or the progressive, on the other hand, even as he tears down the old order, shouts: "Yes!" This is why, in the previous century, revolutionaries so willingly became bureaucrats. They do not oppose fundamental structures of society and the state, but only seek to transform them, to put them into a novel arrangement. The only true enemy of the state is the reactionary, because he fundamentally denies the basis of its validity. [*ETIS* 243]

12. **To be a reactionary is to understand that man is a problem without a human solution.**

It is not unreasonable to suggest that individualism, as an extension of mankind's self-worship, is the defining characteristic of the modern. Chesterton reminds us that the credo of the modern world runs something like this: "That man will get on; he believes in himself" (9). Not only is it mistaken to think that man's self-confidence leads to success, happiness, *et cetera*; in fact, the opposite is the case. Self-confidence leads directly to delusion. Chesterton:

> It would be much truer to say that a man will certainly fail, because he believes in himself. Complete self-confidence is not merely a sin; complete self-confidence is a weakness. Believing utterly in one's self is a hysterical and superstitious belief. (10)

Modern man believes in himself because he has destroyed the idea that there exists anything that is more deserving of his belief and confidence. After all, looking back over a history of innumerable mistakes and catastrophes, what possible evidence could there be for mankind believing in itself? Man can believe in God or nothing. [*ETIS* 381]

13. **The readers of a reactionary author never know if they should applaud with enthusiasm or stamp with rage.**

The leftist is not altogether wrong to warn against reading reactionary books. Indeed, the readers of such books are placed in an uncomfortable position. Upon encountering the timeless truths that emerge through the pages, the reader receives a shock of recognition and a sensation of deep familiarity. In his deepest soul, the same words have resonated long before and he knows not from whence they came. Everyone in modern society has the sneaking suspicion that they have been lied to, that the narratives which structure their lives and thoughts are wrong, but as society repeatedly and vigorously affirms those narratives, they abandon their questions and doubts. The conditioning of modern man is very powerful and thus he feigns outrage so as not to alienate himself from others. Nevertheless, the allure of reactionary authors continues to be strong, especially among those who denounce them the loudest. [*ETIS* 322]

14. The reactionary is not a nostalgic dreamer who yearns for the eradicated past, but rather a hunter of sacred shadows upon the eternal hills.

It is customary to caricature the reactionary position by claiming that it vainly wishes to turn back the clock to some previous era in human history. And for some false representatives of this position, that might be true (in which case, they are deserving of derision). What is less commonly understood—and what Gómez Dávila sought to make clear in his essay "The Authentic Reactionary"—is that it is not the previous forms of human society in and of themselves that we long for, but the expressions of *eternal* truths that were found in them. It is not the particular beauties of the past that we are oriented toward, but the thing that made them beautiful. The source of that beauty remains for us to find because it is not bound by historical contingency. The form should not be confused with the essence. The age of the aristocrat, the monarch, and the peasant has passed out of history and any attempt to restore it could only end in disaster. Furthermore, one need not be a leftist in order to recognize how often the aristocracies and monarchs of the world failed to live up to their ideals. What the authentic reactionary seeks to reinvigorate, even if it is only in his own life, are the principles that animated and inspired the very best of humanity in every age, and which the modern world is predicated on denying. Far from hating humanity, the reactionary passionately loves its capacity for beauty and goodness so much that he cannot bear to see it degraded. [*ETIS* 324]

15. **A reactionary is whoever is not willing to buy his victory at any price.**

For the authentic reactionary, defeat or even death is not the worst that can happen. Although it may seem inconceivable to the modern mentality, he is one for whom honor and dignity are worth more than victory or life. This is because within those concepts that are so outmoded, is contained an entire worldview, a cosmological vision, which the reactionary is unwilling to betray. Victory or defeat occurs according to the turning of the wheel of fortune and any man who will stop at nothing to win only does so because he does not realize the consequences of his actions. It is easier to bear the burden of losing than it is to bear the burden of being wrong. For in the case of the former, one only has to suffer external degradation, but in the case of the latter, finding itself built upon an unstable foundation, the soul collapses in on itself. [*ETIS* 294]

16. **The intelligent man quickly comes to reactionary conclusions. Today, however, the universal consensus of fools frightens him. When they interrogate him in public, he denies being a Galilean.**

The studious observer of history and human nature has little difficulty recognizing the truths that characterize the reactionary position. The fact, however, that it is a position derided, without exception, by society forces him to choose between being ostracized and reviled or renouncing his beliefs. There are few who can face such condemnation with courage and conviction. It is much easier to conform to the stupidities of the modern world and find one's opinions validated and celebrated. If we are going to be wrong, then at least we can find some comfort in knowing that everyone else is wrong too. [*ETIS* 223]

17. The reactionary's ideal is not an earthly paradise, but rather a society similar to that which existed in those calmer periods of ancient European history, of Old Europe, before the demographic, industrial, and democratic catastrophe.

Utopian thinking, whether of the progressive or conservative variety, is foolishness. The reactionary is therefore obliged to take a melancholic posture. It is not a perfect world he awaits with the feverish trembling anticipation of the fanatic. He does not desire a return to the garden of Eden, to a world with no pain or death or struggle. He simply and quietly laments the loss of beauty and nobility, which, not too long ago, could still be found on the earth. The reactionary speaks with the same tones of anguish as those heard in Edmund Burke's voice when, in his *Reflections on the Revolution in France*, he spoke of the death of Marie Antoinette:

> I thought ten thousand swords must have leaped from their scabbards to avenge even a look that threatened her with insult. But the age of chivalry is gone. That of sophisters, economists, and calculators has succeeded; and the glory of Europe is extinguished for ever. (76) [*ETIS* 470]

18. The reactionary does not yearn for the futile restoration of the past, but for the admittedly unlikely rupture of the future with the squalid present.

The fantasy of restoration is simply the inverse of the fantasy of progress. Both are the product of an inadequate understanding of history. The pieces of the old order, irrevocably shattered, will not be reassembled. There is no institution now existing that is worthy of being preserved, not even the Church and certainly not the aristocracies or monarchies, which are as surely outmoded as the dinosaurs. All previous forms of order have lapsed. For the authentic reactionary, however, in contrast to the conservative, hope is to be found in revelation, in the spontaneous and cataclysmic bursting forth of the divine and the sacred into the profane world. This is why the godly man awaits apocalypse in the posture of a beggar seeking alms. Apocalypse, the rending of the veil, can be nothing other than hierophany. We must accept, however, that we are waiting for a miracle, unforeseen and unexpected, an event that we have no ability to hasten or bring to fruition. Like Walter Benjamin's messiah, revelation is an interruption. Every moment is a door through which He may enter. [*ETIS* 224]

19. **Today's reactionary has the satisfaction—which yesterday's did not—of seeing the projects of modernity end not only in ruin, but also in ridicule.**

It seems like only yesterday that science-fiction writers promised us a future of interstellar exploration and colonization. For the reactionary of the past, the future was much more frightening than it is now because we didn't realize how inaccurate those predictions would end up being. The first man on the moon was more than half a century ago and instead of being the beginning of mankind's glorious interstellar future, it seems that it was a one-off. We reactionaries can take comfort in knowing that the climate crisis or some other man-made disaster will likely prevent us from ever having flying cars or Martian colonies. And in the meantime, we can have a few laughs every time their rockets fail to make it off the ground. [*ETIS* 358]

20. **The most convinced reactionary is the repentant revolutionary, that is to say: one who has been intimately acquainted with the reality of the problems and has been exposed to the falsity of the solutions.**

To say that the contemporary Left has become disillusioned or dispirited is putting it mildly. There seems to be an enormous number of leftists nowadays who are either abandoning the leftist project altogether or steering their conception of leftism into uncharted water, for which they are not unreasonably being accused of betrayal by their erstwhile comrades. It is likely that in short order leftism will either become completely outmoded or become totally unrecognizable. None of this is surprising. Climate change and the precipitous decline of democratic institutions and of society as a whole, have demonstrated how ill-equipped leftism is to cope with challenges. The paranoid conservative who sees subversives and communists lurking in every nook and cranny hasn't the faintest idea of how bankrupt the principles of leftism have become. To the leftist, it is painfully clear. He is in the unenviable position of seeing his prognosis become more accurate by the day, while his solutions become more futile and misguided. The working classes, crushed beneath the yoke of economic oppression, distracted by technology, despairing of political change, and terrified of global climate collapse, have neither the energy nor the motivation to rise up. Of course, we know better than to suggest that it would result in anything positive even if they did. [*ETIS* 352]

21. **The reactionary does not turn into a conservative except in ages in which there remains something worthy of being conserved.**

The conservative position at this moment is utterly incoherent. There is no legislation that could possibly restore what has been lost. Fighting for prayer in school is the height of absurdity given the nature of our prayers, our schools, and our lives. Arguing about gender roles is idiotic in a world where a man's only way to provide for his family is to sit in an office building for eight hours a day. In this society, no trace of the glorious ages of the past remains. The rupture between the modern world and the traditional has been fundamental. It is not within human power to resurrect a world that has passed out of history, nor would it be desirable to do so if it were. The conservative may resemble the reactionary insofar as what he yearns for, but unlike the latter, he is deluded and refuses to acknowledge the truth of the world he sees around him. The reactionary knows that the eternal truths can only be recovered within the individual soul, where all things are possible. The conservative mistakenly believes that he can bring his dream into the external world. [*ETIS* 160]

22. **If the Left continues adopting, one after another, the objections that we reactionaries have raised against the modern world, we will have to become leftists.**

When it comes down to it, the principal opposition to the modern world has always come from reactionaries. Romanticism, with some minor exceptions, was not a progressive ideology. From its infancy, anything we might call the leftist project has been on the side of the utopian, the universal, the democratic, and the rational. Nevertheless, as time goes on, the leftist critique, on the surface, begins to resemble that of the reactionary. Realizing the consequences of the modern world, the leftist tries to reposition himself against it, ignoring the fact that leftism itself is entirely a product of that world. We are seeing a realignment of Left and Right at this late stage. We now find leftists fighting on the side of technological automation and state surveillance, and rightists warning against soil erosion and genetically modified food. Increasingly, the lines are not being drawn according to twentieth-century definitions of proletarian and bourgeois, capitalist and communist, or Democrat and Republican—but according to who stands on the side of the modern world and who stands against it. [*ETIS* 374]

23. **Though he knows he cannot win, the reactionary refuses to lie.**

As Michael Warren Davis writes in *The Reactionary Mind*:

> The reactionary isn't interested in beating his opponents, but in winning them over. He has something that they need, and he wants to share it with them: happiness. A good life. Reactionaries don't argue; they act. They lead by example. This is the reactionary imperative. We say that his whole existence is an act of defiance, and so it is. But it's also an invitation. (201)

Although Davis's sentiments here are rather too sanguine for our tastes, he is correct in gesturing toward the disdain for sophistry that characterizes an understanding of the reactionary position that accords with Gómez Dávila. The type of persuasive, clever argumentation that is so frequently used to gather supporters to one's cause is, to Gómez Dávila, dishonest and deceitful. The authentic reactionary will not betray the truth, even to save his life. Montaigne, as usual, puts it best: "I would rather let an affair run to ruin than twist my words to further it" (207). [*ETIS* 166]

24. **The leftist who protests equally against the crimes of the Right or the Left is called a reactionary by his comrades, and with good reason.**

The leftist paragon wants to win, above all else. Whatever horrors are committed by his side are irrelevant as long as they lead to ultimate victory. There certainly are leftists who refuse to turn a blind eye to these horrors and condemn their authors as false betrayers. In so doing, however, they sacrifice their victory, and thereby inspire the scorn and fury of their fellows. Rather than accepting the fact that Stalin and Mao abandoned the path of revolution, the leftists prefer to crucify those that stayed true to their principles. This is because the ultimate leftist principle is to win at all costs, while the principle of the reactionary is to accept losing with grace and dignity. A leftist who resigns himself to defeat is no longer a true leftist. [*ETIS* 268]

IX
The Soul

1. **The soul is man's task.**

If the soul is not well fed, it does not matter how robust the health of the body. If the soul withers, there is no cultivation of the intellect that may enliven. If the soul is dead, there is no wealth that can restore it. Modern man exclusively conceives of his goals and ambitions in material terms. In material terms, modern man lives in a veritable paradise. Even the most wretched slum-dweller has access to resources unimaginable to the feudal serf in times of hardship or famine. And yet the starving medieval peasant, alone in the barren wilderness, suffering from cold and exposure, had a gift that is worth more than the accumulated riches of the capitalists of today: he had a soul that shone forth as brightly as a star in the night sky. There is no mistake about it, the purpose of humanity is not to accumulate possessions or be well fed and comfortable, or even to achieve wisdom and learning or power. We have one purpose, one goal: to gently tend and shelter and feed the tiny flicker of flame within us, which was bestowed to us by God, and which burns forth in the same degree from within all of His creation. [*ETIS* 102]

2. **One who boasts of "having lived through a lot" ought to remain silent lest he demonstrate how little he has understood.**

It is an unfortunate fact that experience, more often than not, fails to confer wisdom. One can just as easily learn nothing at all from a lifetime of experience. Montaigne writes: "[W]hen reason fails us, we make use of experience" (343). In fact, experience is more likely to make a fool confident in his foolishness. We moderns suffer much from a lack of ignorance. One rarely meets a man today who, as Martial put it, "is glad to be what he is, and wishes to be nothing else" (cited in Montaigne, 360) Without knowledge, goodwill, and boldness, experience can teach us nothing. [*ETIS* 353]

3. **Today the individual has to reconstruct within himself the civilized world that is disappearing around him.**

When William Butler Yeats threw himself into the cause of Irish nationalism, he quickly discovered that the Ireland he longed to bring into existence was one that could not possibly exist. In a speech given in New York City in 1904, he describes his vision of Ireland, which represented, in every sense, an alternative to modern industrial England: "In Ireland alone among the nations that I know you will find, away on the Western seaboard, under broken roofs, a race of gentlemen keep alive the ideals of a great time when men sang the heroic life with drawn swords in their hands" (cited in Ellmann, *Yeats*, 116). What was at stake for Yeats, then, in his nationalist project, was nothing less than the revitalization of the heroic golden age. Unsurprisingly, his nationalism rapidly became embittered and disillusioned. Yeats was not wrong to abandon his goal of fighting for a free Ireland, when it became clear that such an Ireland was, in fact, destined to be the same as every other modern European nation. The modern world destroys our dreams, which is why those who resist it find refuge only in dreams and poetry and prayer. [*ETIS* 332]

4. **False elegance is preferable to authentic vulgarity. One who dwells in an imaginary palace demands more from himself than one who is satisfied with a shack.**

Accepting oneself, as we have said previously, means nothing if the self that is accepted is wretched and degenerate. This type of self-satisfaction, Nietzsche observes, is abhorrent to one who is noble. In *Beyond Good and Evil*, he writes:

> Among the things which a noble human being perhaps finds hardest to understand is vanity: he will be tempted to deny its existence where a different type of human being will think it palpably evident. For him the problem is to imagine creatures who try to awaken a good opinion of themselves which they themselves do not hold—and thus do not "deserve" either—and yet nevertheless subsequently come to *believe* this good opinion themselves. (261)

In other words, the man who pretends holds himself to a higher standard than the man who is content. The pretentious man, at least, strives to be greater. [*ETIS* 347]

5. **The soul grows inwardly.**

In the fairy lore of the Celtic Irish, there is an idea that the universe expands paradoxically as it decreases in size. Nestled inside the world, like a Russian doll, are progressively smaller but increasingly more expansive regions. The landscape of the soul is similar. As we travel further and further within, we find immeasurably vast territories. The perceptible immensity of the external world, on the other hand, merely disguises its shallowness. The soul grows by contraction and diminishes through expansion. [*ETIS* 35]

6. **Love is not a mystery, but the space where mystery is dissolved.**

The inexperienced reader of Gómez Dávila may be initially surprised to discover how heavily he valued sexual love. The image of the detached sage, surrounded by books, tends not to be associated with sensual passion. The fact remains, however, that Gómez Dávila consistently emphasizes the virtues of love and sex. His marriage was by all accounts a happy one and we can perceive in instances like the above, for example, his deeply held belief that love was a means of connecting with the divine. Love leads to clarity and understanding. It is the realm where contradictions and paradox are resolved, where the cacophony of life evaporates into a peaceful silence. [*ETIS* 74]

7. **Modern man has no inner life; he barely even has inner conflicts.**

To paraphrase Yeats: hatred of God leads to God. Modern man has largely abdicated all struggles. The turmoil that has, throughout history, led to some of the greatest products of human genius, is absent in modern man. The confrontation between self and soul cannot occur where the latter is presumed not to exist at all. The wistful figures of the paintings of Caspar David Friedrich are completely alien to modern man, who does not understand why they are sitting among ruins, gazing into the twilight. The melancholic and contemplative attitude elicits bewilderment and scorn in someone who is only accustomed to staring at their screens. As material considerations come to dominate modern man, he begins to exist, or to perceive his existence, only in material terms. After more than a century of neglecting and disregarding his inner life, modern man becomes increasingly shallow and superficial. [*ETIS* 420]

8. **In solitude man recovers the strength to live.**

Attempts to engage with modern society are exhausting. In such a profane and degraded world, any contact is bound to be harmful. Seeing the state of things, one wonders why one bothers at all. In the home, however, among one's family or alone, in a little corner of the world, insulated as much as possible from the ongoing calamities of society and the planet, one remembers what is important in life and gradually replenishes one's vitality until one is ready to sally forth once again to the grocery store or the department of motor vehicles. [*ETIS* 412]

9. **The modern poet is a farmer who hopelessly sows a plot of eroded soil.**

The poets of the modern world have largely floundered. The mind, which can never allow something good to remain untouched by its grasping, will probe ceaselessly, always seeking to amend what it has found, cheapening it by its efforts. Not only is there nothing new to be said, every attempt to mine wisdom for every last scrap of value has the effect of diminishing it. As Montaigne notes:

> Who would not say that commentaries increase doubt and ignorance, since there is no book to be found, human or divine, with which the world has any business, in which the difficulties are cleared up by the interpretation? The hundredth commentator passes it on to his successor in a thornier and more crabbed state than that in which the first discovered it. When did we ever agree in saying: "This book has had enough. There is nothing more to be said about it"? (347)

Needless to say, we do not presume to exempt ourselves from this indictment, for, given that modern man has nothing whatsoever to say—what can we do but tinker and rob those hallowed graves of their treasures? [*ETIS* 387]

10. The hand that does not dare to caress cannot know how to write.

The spiritual wisdom of Gómez Dávila's words is not one that denies the sensuous and bodily world. The dour ascetic severity is nowhere to be found in these pages. Even the hermits and recluses that appear here are of a different sort, jovial in their own way and content in their solitude. One has to imagine them well-provided and satisfied. Surely, one cannot write or think without knowing how to love, since the proper motivation for thought and writing in the first place can only be love for the world. Here we are reminded by Montaigne, who writes:

> I who boast of embracing the pleasures of life so eagerly and so deliberately, find in them, when I consider them so minutely, little more than wind. But what of that? We are all wind. And the wind itself, wiser than we, takes pleasure in blustering and veering round, and is content with its own functions. It does not desire stability or solidity, qualities that do not belong to it. (395)

It is, therefore, as much in our natures to enjoy as it is to disdain, and there is nothing in the life of Gómez Dávila to suggest that he thought otherwise. [*ETIS* 287]

11. In the last corner of the labyrinth of the soul, there grunts a frightened ape.

There is good reason for modern man to avoid anything that will cause him to look within himself. Modern culture—the stories we surround ourselves with—allows us to preserve the idea that we are more than what we are. The soul becomes a secret boarded-up room that we refuse to open because it is the place where we have stowed away all of our deepest fears. We try to forget its existence because we know what's in there and we know what it would mean if we saw the grisly evidence we have hidden inside: we would no longer be able to maintain the fantasy that we are godlike supermen. We would no longer be able to pretend that we are powerful, that we can control the world. We would see ourselves for the small, weak, pitiful beings that we truly are. And the modern world could not survive for one moment longer if we did so. [*ETIS* 341]

12. **The punishment of the man who searches for himself is that he finds himself.**

The quest of the modern age is man's quest to discover himself. Having lost his true identity, modern man desperately tries to see past the disenchanted quotidian world that surrounds him, in the hope that his true essence will reveal his true nature as some sort of liberated divine being. This realization, he expects, will deliver him from his suffering. He will be able to rise above his circumstances and fulfill his grand destiny. Search, however, and you shall surely find. The culmination of this quest will not be a happy one for man. For after all the searching and questing, what he finds at the end of his journey is a weak, limited, and ignorant being, who is shackled to his condition, to his circumstances, and, above all, to history. He cannot become whatever he desires; he can only be what he is. In the end, man has no recourse unto himself, but only unto God and the sacred. [*ETIS* 165]

13. **Meditation is dialogue with the dead.**

To clear the mind, to silence the infernal din of the modern world, to be still within the self is to enter the timeless world, to be surrounded by ghosts. Where do the dead live, if not within our souls? In its deepest, most remote places, the soul is densely populated by the spirits of the dead. When we close our minds to the distracting noise emanating from the external world, we become sensitive to the voices of these dead. The calm that descends upon man in moments of meditation is the product of listening to what is timeless and eternal. The sound of the heartbeat, the rhythm of the breath, speaks in the language of what has been lost. It is the memory of wakefulness. It is the lion's roar, summoning us to rise from our insipid modern dreams. [*ETIS* 126]

14. **Our soul has a future. Humanity has none.**

Insofar as forms are, by definition, transitory, we can see that humanity, deprived of that which connects it to the timeless and eternal, is destined to perish. The means of liberating mankind from so-called superstition through reason, in denying the soul, has doomed us. The consequence of the modern mentality has been to sever us from that within us which is essential and, in this world of universal degradation and impoverishment, we are beginning to see the result come to fruition. A soulless humanity cannot survive. [*ETIS* 255]

15. **A cultured soul is one in which the cacophony of the living does not drown out the music of the dead.**

The modern world, to adapt a phrase from Chesterton, exclusively privileges the voices of the living minority by silencing the neglected majority: the dead. We live in this world, yes, but if we attune ourselves to the voices of the dead, we can still find, amongst all the vulgarity and degradation of the present, the beauty of that which has passed away. When we allow the pressing concerns of modern society to somewhat fade into the background, we enter the timeless realm. The fact that the living voices are louder and more urgent should not confuse us into thinking that they are more important. [*ETIS* 205]

16. **Those who release man from his chains are only liberating an animal.**

Just as chains can only restrain humanity in its most basic, limited, and external nature, to free humanity from its chains likewise can only provide the most basic, limited, and external freedom. Man is more than his external, biological reality. As long as we focus only on the outward conditions of man, we cannot substantively perceive or address what he truly is, nor can we do anything for him. [*ETIS* 161]

17. **Lyric poetry survives because the heart is the only place where reason fears to tread.**

We are lucky that reason is not as powerful as modern man thinks it is. It is true that reason is a voracious and cruel beast that devours everything it can. Reason can turn our greatest joys into sorrows. Like a colony of termites, it can hollow out something beautiful and full of life, leaving only a dessicated husk. Through the pitiless lens of reason, the cosmos, once thought of as alive and vibrant, is reconceived as a mere arrangement of materials. And yet the dominion of reason is not uncontested. There are realms where reason is consistently and vigorously defied; landscapes so inhospitable to reason that it fails to make significant inroads. Though reason excels in adapting itself, there are languages with which it is fundamentally incompatible—namely, the languages of the heart and the soul. Wracked by awesome tempests and populated by wild, ungovernable and shadowy entities, reason finds no purchase upon the savage shores of the heart's realm. [*ETIS* 106]

18. **The realm of the imagination is the only place in the world where it is possible to dwell.**

The modern spirit—or the Faustian spirit, as Spengler puts it—expands outwardly. Colonialism, industrialism, capitalism, are all oriented toward growth and expansion: more land, more resources, more financial markets. Modern man always looks toward the horizon, toward what is beyond, and the center is lost. Ernst Jünger, grounded in the study of biology, observed that organisms are most perfected in their most basic and least differentiated state. A single-celled being is complete in itself. As we grow limbs and expand outward, we become severed from perfection. This is why, Jünger says, the posture of the Buddha is one in which all the limbs are folded and contracted inward (45). As we move inward, we grow toward perfection, wholeness, and the totality. [*ETIS* 184]

19. **It is only possible to support the weight of this world by kneeling.**

Modern man likes to imagine himself as the titan Atlas, who carries the world on his shoulders. This heroic pose may suit a superhuman titan but, for man, the weight of our burden crushes us to the ground. Those who think themselves strong enough to stand will be brought low. It is only in a posture of humility and reverence that we find the strength to bear this terrible gravity. [*ETIS* 424]

X
Nature

1. **One who recalls the smells of grass trampled beneath his bare feet never breathes well among buildings.**

It is undeniably trite to say so, but there is magic in the world. Every child knows it. Yeats knew it, Chesterton knew it, and Gómez Dávila knew it. Magic is alive in the colors of the leaves, in the rising of the sun, and in the smell of grass. Chesterton observes that

> this world does not explain itself. It may be a miracle with a supernatural explanation; it may be a conjuring trick, with a natural explanation. But the explanation of the conjuring trick, if it is to satisfy me, will have to be better than the natural explanations I have heard. (66)

The scientific explanation of the world fails utterly to account for the miraculous and the magical. And as science denies the magical nature of the world, modern man constructs a world that conforms to this disenchanted vision. If he can no longer understand magic, he will ensure that magic is driven from the world. Once again, Chesterton: "[T]here had come into my mind a vague and vast impression that in some way all good was a remnant to be stored and held sacred out of some primordial ruin" (66). [*ETIS* 382]

2. **The pollution of the conceptual world by the modern mentality is more harmful than the pollution of the environment by modern industry.**

Environmentalists and ecologists have almost without exception failed to account for the reasons for man's brutal exploitation of nature and his utter disregard for the consequences. The truth is that modern man is given no reason to care about nature. If the most compelling argument in favor of living in harmony with the natural world is that it will benefit humanity, then the climate catastrophe should come as no surprise, for there is nothing so constant as man's tendency to act against his own best interest. Modern man is so hopeless and suicidal that he will not act to prevent his own destruction. As far as the argument that "nature" is an "other" that deserves respect or, worse yet, rights, we need only look to see how little man is invested in extending respect to his fellow human beings and how eagerly he is willing to deprive them of rights. The only compelling reason for the preservation of nature is its fundamental divinity, so in an age when the concept of divinity is meaningless, there can be no hope for the natural world or, for that matter, the human world. Nature was not protected in ages past by man's superior understanding of planetary systems, but by his conviction that nature was divine. [*ETIS* 379]

3. **The joyful path is traveled barefoot.**

The simple pleasures of the child continue to gesture toward the nature of happiness. To walk in the untroubled manner of the child is to walk with joy. Chesterton says that he learned the totality of his philosophy in the nursery. He writes:

> Modern minor poets are naturalists, and talk about the bush or the brook; but the singers of the old epics and fables were supernaturalists, and talked about the gods of brook and bush. That is what the moderns mean when they say that the

> ancients did not "appreciate Nature," because they said that nature was divine. Old nurses do not tell children about the grass, but about the fairies that dance on the grass; and the old Greeks could not see the trees for the dryads. (49)

When we walk barefoot, in the manner of those fairies and dryads, we walk in an enchanted world. The modern world, in contrast, denies the fantastic wildness of nature, which, in turn, denies the necessity of adopting a posture of reverence and humility in the face of it. If the child walks barefoot, so does the penitent. [*ETIS* 341]

4. **A thought should not expand symmetrically like a formula, but wildly like a shrub.**

It is unclear which has suffered more from the scientific mechanistic modern vision: our image of the cosmos or our image of ourselves. If the universe is nothing but a clockwork mechanism, then we can be nothing but cogs and gears. If nature is seen as passive and tractable, then that is how we come to see ourselves as well. In this context it is not surprising that human thought should have become so impoverished. As the human mind is essentially a mirror image of nature and the cosmos, the creative force should be properly seen as explosive and disordered, sending out tendrils and bursting forth buds and shoots hither and thither. It is the job of the gardener to come in later to prune them. [*ETIS* 347]

5. **The widely touted "dominion of man over nature" has turned out to be merely an immense capacity for murder.**

As climate change is making abundantly clear, mankind cannot control nature. After two centuries, the biosphere has been so radically devastated that even if we immediately stopped emitting any carbon whatsoever, the global systems that make the earth hospitable to human life would not recover. Mankind declared victory over nature prematurely. We can certainly drive animals to extinction, clear-cut forests, dig vast mining complexes, and fill the ocean with toxic waste, but have we really managed to bend nature to our will? Are we any better prepared to withstand the storms, heatwaves, and floods than those who came before us? The modern world is more fragile than we know. But we will learn. [*ETIS* 474]

6. **The longer we postpone nature's revenge for the crimes committed against her, the more cruel her vengeance shall be.**

It seems likely that as humanity starts noticing more of the consequences of climate change, the scientists and engineers will start implementing all sorts of high-tech plans to avoid its worst effects. If they fail, millions will perish. If they succeed, we will find that we have lost more by our success than we would have by our failure. Waves, when meeting an obstacle upon the shore, do not dissipate, but regather their strength and return with greater fury until they overwhelm the barrier. Nature will not be thwarted. At best we can delay the inevitable but to do so will, in effect, simply mean twisting the knife. Rather than accepting his fate with dignity, man will make its consequences worse with his incessant and craven attempts to escape it. As the American ecologist Guy McPherson has observed: "Nature bats last." She will always have the last word. [*ETIS* 362]

7. **The mastery that man has gained over nature simply enables him to debase it without fear.**

The tragic fate of nature in the contemporary world is a product of the fact that mankind no longer fears the natural world. In ages past, the threats—both natural and supernatural—that emanated from the dark woods and the wild moors protected nature and demanded of man a reciprocal relationship. Superstition, properly understood, constitutes precisely one such relationship. You may extend up to this point, but not beyond—or there will be dreadful consequences. Modernity, in all senses, abolishes limits and boundaries. In the case of nature, this has meant total destruction. When the borders between the human and natural world are no longer enforceable and respected, humanity drives forward relentlessly like a plague of locusts. In the world of the present, mankind refuses to meet at the negotiating table with nature, and imposes the most extravagant demands, which nature, defanged and cowering, is forced to accept. In the end, however, we have now realized that we will pay the tributes so long overdue and nature will have its revenge. [*ETIS* 259]

8. **Nature, as such, has become extinct in our century. Only in the art of previous centuries do we discover, to our astonishment, that nature is not just a simple physics experiment operated by industrious little organisms.**

The sense of awe and wonder that the natural world has always produced in mankind's breast is a thing of the past. It is not merely the industrial exploitation of the land and the urbanization of the human race that has brought this to pass. The rationalistic and scientific worldview, in order to analyze, must break every phenomenon into fragmentary parts. Given the immeasurable complexity of these phenomena and the inherent limitations of the power of human observation, the result is inevitably the reduction of a rich and profound totality to a mechanical, static relationship between discrete units. Cells, molecules, and particles invariably perform their limited functions, according to perceived and observable principles. The mystery of swirling eddies of water is replaced by a mere sequence of mathematical functions. The miracle of life is reduced to the businesslike collaboration of chemical and physiological agents, their actions no more than the product of their programming. [*ETIS* 187]

9. **We are approaching an age in which nature, displaced by humanity, will only survive in greenhouses and museums.**

Given the rapidly accelerating processes of urbanization and industrial agriculture, the vast majority of the human race essentially lives without ever experiencing nature. In the coming decades seventy-five percent of humanity will live in cities. For these benighted souls, nature will only exist as a distant memory, preserved in the great works of art. Gazing at the works of Arnold Böcklin or Caspar David Friedrich, the man of the future may find some mysterious stirring in some long-forgotten region of his soul. Or he will visit some withered remnant of a tree, preserved like an Incan mummy, in a glass house and wonder uncomprehendingly why it makes him weep. [*ETIS* 180]

10. **I do not yearn for an untouched nature, a nature without the mark of the peasant that ennobles it or the palace that crowns the hill. But for a nature safe from plebeian industrialism and irreverent exploitation.**

It has become popular in some circles to champion a vision of a pure nature of which man is, at best, an undifferentiated component, no different than any other beast. Some go further and imagine that the glory of nature would be even greater if man did not exist at all. Inescapably, however, life is more than a purely biological function. The consciousness of mankind, whether it is a gift or a curse, separates us from the rest of creation. Bestowed with imagination and creativity, man is able to change the world and, more importantly, change himself. Since man cannot alter the fundamental fact of his difference from the rest of nature, therefore, his choice only extends as far as *how* and *in what manner* to interact with nature, not whether or not to do so. While modern man builds shopping malls and factories, medieval man built cathedrals and ancient man built temples. The former degrade and disfigure nature, while the latter, perhaps, accentuate its beauty and draw attention to its sacredness. Premodern man understood that the nature of his relationship to the land and the gods was of paramount importance and his actions toward nature reflect this concern. Modern man sees nature, devoid of higher significance, as nothing more than grist for the mill, which can be indefinitely manipulated and exploited in service of his own perverse desires. [*ETIS* 178]

XI
Aristocracy

1. **Man truly admires only the things that are given without merit: talent, lineage, beauty.**

Why should we admire what we ourselves are capable of doing? To deserve something is the same as to merely have done what is necessary for it to be conferred upon one. Man does not admire those things which are the product of such reciprocity. We admire those things which have been bestowed from God, those things for which we cannot account. This is why there is nothing more deserving of admiration than beauty, which descends inexplicably and miraculously. [*ETIS* 259]

2. **Wisdom consists in moderating oneself not out of fear for excess, but out of love for boundaries.**

What Gómez Dávila is suggesting here is that moderation should be a positive rather than a reactive impulse. All too often we assume that moderation is desirable because we believe that immoderation is unhealthy or brings other negative consequences. Smoking too much tobacco will kill us, for instance, so we try to moderate our consumption in order to avoid that result. This is a fearful reaction, however, and one that often fails. A positive form of moderation is one that derives from an acceptance of the inherent value in limiting and restricting oneself. Moderation should not be an attempt to insulate the self from harm, but a noble and heroic endeavor. The aristocratic soul is forged through self-discipline. In the words of Montaigne: "[T]emperance is the moderator, not the enemy of pleasures." (404) [*ETIS* 34]

3. **To refuse to admire is the mark of the beast.**

Modern man loves to see works of so-called modern art so that he can say to himself: I could do that. Rembrandt, on the other hand, horrifies him because he knows instinctively that even if he had the time, inclination, and training, he would never be able to produce such works of genius. What characterizes Lucifer, if not resentment and envy? There is nothing more noble than to acknowledge something that is utterly beyond us, something before which we stand in awe, in full awareness of our own limitations. The appearance of genius, which is not the product of circumstances or training, has always been understood as a gift from God. To refuse to recognize genius as a unique and privileged condition, which is by definition inaccessible to all, is a blasphemy. [*ETIS* 29]

4. **After seeing work exploit and destroy the world, indolence seems like the mother of virtues.**

The early European explorers were not wrong to identify as idle the people they found in communities as yet untouched by the modern contagion, but they were wrong to condemn it. The revisionist historian who seeks to show how industrious traditional communities truly were does them no favors and only demonstrates how enslaved he is to capitalist notions of value. The Marxist and leftist historians and anthropologists are at least correct in their conclusion that premodern modes of life allowed a much greater degree of leisure for all members of those societies. The demands upon the time of the medieval serf were trivial in comparison to the capitalist laborer, even including the CEO who brings home a seven-figure salary. This is one of the chief virtues of aristocratic society: the valuing of nonproductive activity. The aristocratic order, for Gómez Dávila, was one that encouraged the blossoming forth of the best mankind has to offer. If the ideal man of ages past was wise, sensitive, brave, and cultured, the ideal man of the modern world is an overworked and overstimulated neurotic. [*ETIS* 333]

5. **The ignorant believe that the expression "aristocratic manners" signified insolent conduct; one who actually looks into the subject discovers that the expression signified courtesy, refinement, and dignity.**

Modern man, when he bothers to think about the past at all, imagines the aristocracy to have been some species of vicious parasite, cruelly preying upon the poor. Of course, we believe this because it is exactly how the wealthy behave in our world. How could it have been otherwise in the benighted past, when we lacked even the notion of political liberty? We indict the feudal aristocracy for the crimes of our own heartless and corrupt capitalist overseers. When we actually try to understand the meaning of the aristocracy, however, we are shocked to find that the feudal lords of the past bear little resemblance to the oligarchs of the contemporary world. As Michael Warren Davis puts it:

> Feudalism—as an economic, political, religious, and cultural order—survived for so long because people believed in it; they believed in its values of faithfulness, service, charity, honor, duty, sacrifice, and, most of all, chivalry. They fell short of these values. They fought over them, but they always labored to restore them. (13)

It is easy for the modern liberal historian to dwell on instances of aristocratic excesses and abuses, but harder for him to demonstrate how those with power in capitalist society are in any way preferable. [*ETIS* 455]

6. **For more than a century there has been no upper class. At the most we might say there is a pretentious segment of the middle class.**

It is telling that modern man is only capable of conceptualizing class in economic terms and it is a mistake to associate the historical aristocracy with the wealthy of today. While Gómez Dávila indeed romanticized the aristocracy and was generally elitist in his outlook, he had no loyalty to the rich. Where the feudal aristocracy was bound by obligations and expected to maintain unique values, those at the top of the economic food chain today subscribe to the same bourgeois mentality as the middle class and the poor. There has certainly never been an American aristocracy and even the Southern planter class, which is perhaps the closest historical analog, was entirely defined by economic exploitation rather than a culture or system of values. A true aristocracy is explicitly hostile toward commercial activity, and it structures society by specifically preventing economic mobility. In an aristocratic society, everyone has his place, which is valued and honored, regardless of how much money he has. Under such a system, accumulating wealth is ultimately discouraged because it will not fundamentally change one's place in society. Whether he liked it or not, the aristocrat was born into a role which made strenuous demands upon him that were rigidly enforced. As soon as hereditary class distinctions are abolished, society is consumed by a hysterical compulsion to accumulate capital. Money, in an egalitarian society, is the only thing that matters and the only determinant of man's worth. [*ETIS* 357]

7. **Love of the people is the duty of the aristocrat. The democrat only loves them during election season.**

Despite a lifetime of evidence to the contrary, the myth of the politician continues to exert an influence. Shockingly, one politician is reviled for what he says, while another is celebrated. As though there was any reason whatsoever to think that any of them believes what they say or intends to act based on what they say. The farce has become completely transparent, for which I suppose we have some cause to be thankful. Better by far that people abandon the notion that politicians care for them in any meaningful way, than continue the fantasy that those who govern us are concerned for us. Needless to say, no matter how clear this is to virtually everyone in a society, they will nevertheless perpetuate the narrative that democracy holds an inherent virtue and is the best of all possible political structures. We must, after all, be moving forward! [*ETIS* 28]

8. **In this age of universal embourgeoisement, I yearn less for the dead aristocracy than for the vanished commoners.**

Gómez Dávila's elitism should not be confused with contempt for the poor. His nostalgia for feudalism was inspired by a belief in the proper ordering of society as a hierarchy in which each segment plays a vital and honored role. The peasant, therefore, possesses no less virtue than the nobleman and his contributions to society are just as valuable. For much of modern history, moreover, the preservation of tradition was the domain of the rural poor. In the absence of this integrating structure, however, the poor are reduced to nothing more than resentful proto-bourgeoisie. [*ETIS* 156]

9. **Disdain for "formalities" is clear evidence of imbecility.**

Anyone who has traveled among traditional communities cannot help but notice the profound attention given there to matters of formality. This is not merely a byproduct of their old-fashioned sensibilities. This is the means by which such communities maintain goodwill and cohesion among their members. The way modern man thinks about such things as manners and respect, on the other hand, tells us everything we need to know about our society. To dismiss manners and such courtesies as are superficially classified "formalities" is to announce to the world that one cares little for oneself or others. Vulgarity is slavish. As Nietzsche puts it: "The noble soul has reverence for itself" (*Beyond Good and Evil*, 287). Manners are precisely the way one demonstrates this reverence. Modern man does not take manners seriously, but he is not immune to them in any case. Edmund Burke writes:

> Manners are of more importance than laws. The law can touch us here and there, now and then. Manners are what vex or soothe, corrupt or purify, exalt or debase, barbarize or refine us, by a constant, steady, uniform, insensible operation like that of the air we breathe in. (*Letters on a Regicide Peace*, 66)

There is no situation whatsoever, in which ones' manners and the manners of others do not have an impact. No matter what, manners shape our perceptions of ourselves and others. To ignore manners is simply to have bad manners. [*ETIS* 91]

10. **To be an aristocrat is to believe that not everything depends on the will.**

It is hard not to read here a challenge to Nietzsche's conception of the noble soul or the man of will or the overman. Is not the true aristocrat—Gómez Dávila implicitly argues—the one who accepts that man cannot make himself into something other than what he is? Here we see an example of Gómez Dávila's hostility toward romanticism. Man cannot simply *transform* himself into something he is not. One cannot will beauty, talent, or lineage. Indeed, there is a certain degree of vulgarity in Nietzsche's exhortations to greatness. Montaigne writes:

> It is easier to follow art than nature but it is also much less noble and commendable. The soul's greatness consists not so much in climbing high and pressing forward as in knowing how to adapt and limit itself. It takes all that is merely sufficient as great, and shows its distinction by preferring what is moderate to what is outstanding. (400)

Modern man has lost much of what once made him great by setting his sights higher and higher. The true revolt against the modern way of thinking may lie in accepting ourselves as God and nature formed us, and setting aside our lofty aspirations and striving for mastery. [*ETIS* 93]

11. The genuine aristocrat is one who has an interior life. Regardless of birth, rank, or fortune.

Ernst Jünger found much in Gómez Dávila that was to his liking. Jünger's figure of the "anarch," in particular, bears a striking resemble to Gómez Dávila. Perhaps most importantly, the anarch is defined by a refusal to try to change or improve the society he despises, because he ultimately does not need society or desire to be a part of it. He is untouched by the chaos of historical events and has an infinite recourse to his own interiority. Jünger writes: "his inner strength is far greater. In fact, the anarch's state is the state that each man carries within himself" (82). Like Gómez Dávila, Jünger believes that there is a place within the soul that is impervious and that no matter how oppressive it may become, society "cannot penetrate a man's innermost core" (83). Just as for Gómez Dávila, we can always maintain our inner loyalties in the face of irrevocable and inevitable loss, Jünger's anarch can always find an inner freedom. [*ETIS* 111]

12. **The ruling class of an agrarian society is an aristocracy; that of an industrial society is an oligarchy.**

Whatever charges one may fairly level at the aristocracies of the past—and they are many—it remains that this class sought to represent the best qualities in humanity. This was the goal and the expectation, however often it failed. The numerous codes of conduct that the aristocracy was obligated to follow were designed with this purpose in mind: to cultivate kindness, gentleness, virtue, generosity, strength. Chivalry is most often dismissed nowadays as patronizing and chauvinistic, but we can certainly see that the absence of these high-minded ideals has not prevented the misuse of power or diminished man's capacity for evil—it just encourages the worst in us. The aristocracy stood for something, for a constellation of ideas that represented the best humanity has to offer. The oligarchs and billionaires of modern society are not guided by any principles whatsoever other than profit. They are as wretched as everyone else and don't pretend to be otherwise—they just have a lot more money. [*ETIS* 255]

XII
The Modern World

1. Man does not know what he destroys until after he has destroyed it.

Modern man gazes upon the wreckage he has made of the world with the same kind of incredulity as a child who accidentally broke a window with an errant ball. The fact that humanity had no idea what it was doing shows not that we are evil, but that we are tragic. Evil, or even madness, is rare. Stupidity is universal. [*ETIS* 288]

2. The modern world will not be punished. It is the punishment.

In the face of the countless iniquities of the modern world, it is impossible not to yearn for some kind of divine scourge to come down and wipe our sins away. We rant impotently against the wickedness and horror we see in the hopes that it will somehow be put right. And whether we hope for this deliverance to come from God or man, we are mistaken in our hopes, for the truth of the matter is that the modern world is the instrument of its own destruction. What better cure could there be for the evils of industrialism than climate change? What more effective means could there be for demonstrating the errors of democracy than the plague of authoritarian populism? What more profound illustration of the soullessness of technology than a world where people rot away while staring at their phones? A world where all meaning is created by human interpretation will necessarily become a world of incoherence and despair. We sowed a diseased seed and now we reap a poisoned harvest. [*ETIS* 237]

3. **The modern is the product of an initial act of pride; the modern is that which apparently allows us to escape the human condition.**

At the root, what is this thing that we have called "the modern"? In a word, it is that revolutionary Promethean, Faustian, Luciferian spirit that seeks to make man and his world more than what they are. The modern is hubris, it is pride, it is vanity. It is a disordering, a refusal to accept and submit. It is a denial of powers beyond humanity. It is the most radical form of exceptionalism. It is the deification of mankind and the will. [*ETIS* 454]

4. **It has required enormous effort to make the modern world so ugly.**

We shouldn't make the mistake of thinking that modern man has accomplished nothing. In fact, he has achieved a task so Herculean and titanic that no other age of man could have imagined it: he has made the beautiful, miraculous, divine world into something ugly and hateful. Let us give modern man his fair share of credit: the beauty of this world has not been easy to destroy. Man has had to work hard at his task, day and night for decades and centuries. It has taken the cooperative efforts of billions of people to make this happen. And there have been setbacks and reverses of fortune. Every natural disaster, every flood that washes away shopping centers and mini-mansions, every earthquake that reduces giant concrete towers to rubble, is a victory for the opposition, for beauty. But modern man does not give up and it seems that in our age, we will see the ultimate triumph of ugliness over beauty. [*ETIS* 384]

5. **When it comes down to it, good manners are a way to demonstrate respect. Respect, by the same token, is a way to acknowledge the presence of one's superior. Therefore, whenever hierarchies collapse, good manners die out. Rudeness is a democratic product.**

It's no surprise that in a society where no one and nothing deserves our respect, we likewise find a total absence of good manners. To respect someone is to acknowledge that they are stronger than we are or wiser than we are. If modern society teaches us to refuse to acknowledge that we are not all equal, then on what basis are we expected to show each other respect? Why would I respect someone who is just as ignorant and wretched as myself? Democratic society, which necessarily functions according to the principle of the lowest common denominator, guarantees universal rudeness. [*ETIS* 119]

6. **All non-hierarchical societies are divided into two parts.**

In the absence of more meaningful distinctions, a man's wealth, or lack thereof, is the only quality that matters. The egalitarian reformers have not done away with divisions; they have only made them simplistic and vulgar. We condemn the Hindu caste system or European feudalism as barbaric, but the distance between the modern CEO and the beggar on the street is further than the distance between the king and his humblest subject. [*ETIS* 207]

7. **Bureaucracy is not frightening because it paralyzes, but because it functions.**

As Burckhardt pointed out, the modern world belongs to managers and messenger boys. It is common to suppose that the ills of society are due to the mismanagement or misapplication of the systems modern man has imposed upon the world. When it is criticized, bureaucracy is criticized primarily for being inefficient, for bogging down the political, civic, and economic institutions that it inhabits. What this critique overlooks is the fact that bureaucracy performs its purpose perfectly. Its goal is precisely that stultifying effect it so admirably produces. In a world that is conceived as the sum of myriad component parts to be managed and organized by dispassionate rationality, life itself in its vibrant, joyful abundance is a threat. The more efficient the bureaucratic system, the more inhospitable it is to life. [*ETIS* 181]

8. **The modern world bitterly censures those who "turn their back on life." But what if turning one's back on life is to turn one's face toward the light?**

Modern society is possessive and jealous. It excuses a seemingly limitless number of crimes, but fiercely condemns anyone who expresses the slightest inclination to not be a part of it. This is telling. Like a patient suffering from Stockholm syndrome, modern man is allowed to contemplate anything except the identity of his captor. The only thing worse than being a part of modern society, we are taught, is not being a part of modern society. [*ETIS* 158]

9. **The carelessness with which contemporary humanity is squandering its goods suggests that it does not expect to have any descendants.**

For all the apocalyptic fears that climate change has inspired among the public and for all the ambitious plans to avert its most devastating impacts, modern humanity, from its actions, appears to have resigned itself to near-term extinction. Biologically, it seems from plummeting fertility and birthrates that we already know what so many of us refuse to accept: the last generations of humanity must presently be at hand. No one can any longer claim ignorance of the consequences of carbon emissions, deforestation, and so on, and yet among the people there seems to be no sense of urgency whatsoever. There is no conspiracy to keep us uninformed; everything is happening in plain sight. The conclusion then is inescapable that modern humanity is prepared to die. [*ETIS* 334]

10. **All peace is paid for with vileness.**

For decades, neoliberal capitalism has managed to create peace, generally speaking, in the world. And what was the price we paid for it? Rampant environmental, social, and economic devastation. Peace and justice or peace and happiness have very little to do with each other. The cost of war is great, but few in the modern world are willing to recognize that the cost of peace is greater still. Traditional communities have always understood that a constant low level of warfare is instrumental in preventing total domination, which, in the end, is exactly what peace means. [*ETIS* 124]

11. **Modern conflicts arise more from the desire to suppress conflict than from the desire to defeat an enemy. Plunder, ideology, or adventure has motivated fewer wars in our time than the utopian dream of peace.**

The violent escapades of our ancestors were of a radically different nature than those of the modern world. As Pierre Clastres and others have sought to demonstrate, war, in a premodern context, served many vital functions—the resistance to hegemony perhaps chief among them. Communities locked together in war resist the accumulation and centralization of power. Victory does not bring a cessation of hostilities. Notions of valor and honor necessitate never-ending feuds, which facilitate a balancing of powers. Such a state of war brings communities together, as Karl Jaspers observed: "The teacher of love teaches struggle; the teacher of loveless isolation from the world teaches serenity" (*Psychologie der Weltanschauungen*, 110). Here we can perceive the profoundly existential dimensions of war, battle, and combat. One need only think of Ernst Jünger to see war as a method of gaining self-knowledge.

Now we have a hegemony more total than the Roman emperors could have ever imagined in their wildest fantasies. And as war can only serve to disrupt hegemony, the wars of the modern world are consistently motivated by the preservation of an imbalanced status quo. In fact, even to call them "wars" misses the point entirely. They are better understood as policing actions. Armed conflict in the twenty-first century is almost without exception asymmetrical. One force seeks to maintain its supremacy, while another, which is destined for defeat, attempts to resist. The modern imperium demands peace, which requires uniformity and conformity, and the punishment for refusal brings with it the might of the most devastating weapons of war ever devised by man. The number of victims given to the blood-drenched gods of war is doubtless eclipsed many times over by those offered in sacrifice to the modern dream of peace. [*ETIS* 131]

12. The egalitarian is exasperated when he sees that compulsory education only eliminates perceived inequality in favor of intensifying innate inequality.

Mandatory education does not eliminate the distinctions between the genius and the fool, which forces us to ask the question: Where does the source of inequality truly lie? Two students will receive the exact same education and yet one will excel while the other will fail. The progressive cannot accept the fact that natural inequalities exist. If compulsory education does not eradicate inequality, then the progressive merely pivots to the next set of circumstances: racial, economic, and so on. He will always be searching for the key that will explain why people are different so he can abolish it with all due haste and make them all the same. [*ETIS* 247]

13. **As the floodwaters of this age rise, delicate and noble sentiments, sensuous and refined tastes, and discreet and profound ideas find sanctuary in a few isolated souls, just as the survivors of the deluge took refuge on the peaks of remote mountains.**

Just like the ancestral gods of the Irish Celts diminished in size and power as Christianity displaced them, until they were forced to retreat into their underground halls, truth and beauty flee from the catastrophe of the modern world. Truth and beauty have no home in our society; they are fugitives, enemies of all that now exists. Dishonesty, cruelty, degeneracy, and ugliness reign supreme here and they jealously guard their possessions. Wherever something beautiful, kind or gentle, or truthful emerges in this society it is, at best, dismissed and ignored. At worst it is condemned, persecuted, and punished. It is only among those sheltered few, who manage to keep their heads above the water, who persist in preserving the eternal tradition amidst the ruins of this impoverished world, that truth and beauty find safe haven. We must honor this sacred trust and be the guardians and stewards of the divine truth until the floodwaters recede and the world is born anew. [*ETIS* 151]

14. **Everything that can be reduced to a system ends up in the hands of fools.**

Here we may detect a similar sentiment in one of Nietzsche's "Maxims and Arrows" from *Twilight of the Idols*: "I mistrust all systematizers and avoid them. The will to a system is a lack of integrity" (26).

What is a system if not a method for eliminating complexity in order to be more easily understood? We develop systems so that we can continue to manipulate things that we do not understand. The system is clear, it has definable parameters, it functions predictably, it can be effectively utilized with minimal training. The easier something is to use or understand, the more suitable and desirable it is for modern society. Accepting that modern society is never going to be less likely to produce more and more fools, we do what we can to ensure that stupidity is never an obstacle to success. [*ETIS* 457]

15. **In order to scandalize anyone today it is enough to suggest that he renounce something.**

When people hear that my family and I do not own cell phones or have the Internet at home, they are shocked. In that shock lies a host of emotions and assumptions. Their first impulse is to laugh as if they had been confronted by a gallery of carnival freaks. Humor is a natural response to oddity and abnormality. Laughter seems to be followed by genuine confusion. Is it possible to live without these things? How could such a person function? Then, inevitably, some form of memory returns to them. They had forgotten that they ever lived without having all their experiences mediated through an intrusive omniscient technology. This sudden recollection ends on a wistful note. "That must be nice. I wish I could do that," they often say, never thinking that such a renunciation lies within their power. How crazy would it be to suggest to someone that they should live without electricity or running water? Without a car? Without any of the myriad comforts and conveniences with which we moderns have surrounded ourselves? Throughout history those who have sought union with the divine have done so through renunciation. But when the idea of divinity itself, much less some kind of communion with it, is denied, renunciation appears to be the act of a madman. [*ETIS* 392]

16. The classical humanities educate because they ignore the most basic assumptions of modern consciousness.

An education in the humanities is frequently derided in modern society for being irrelevant. Why should somebody in this society bother to study Shakespeare or Virgil? This is exactly why the humanities and the classics are essential: because they have nothing to do whatsoever with modernity. The wisdom and beauty of Horace or Dante is fundamentally at odds with the way people think in modern society. Wisdom, beauty, and sacrality are all alien concepts to modern man. The philistines are precisely correct that in order to be successful in this society one has no use for such things. Frankly, there is no point teaching anything in this society other than accounting or air-conditioner repair. [*ETIS* 458]

17. The taste of the masses is characterized not by their hostility toward the good, but by the passivity with which they enjoy equally the good, the mediocre, and the bad.
The masses do not have bad taste. They simply do not have taste.

Really bad taste is nowadays as rare as genuinely good taste and is somehow even more impressive an achievement. The primary reason the masses enjoy the drivel that Hollywood pumps out is that it is what has been placed in front of them. They will consume whatever they are given with the same bland ambivalence. In essence, the issue here is an inability or unwillingness to distinguish. The idea of substantive differences in quality is one that is incompatible with modern thought. Without having a sense of a basis upon which to judge the good from the bad, one cannot tell the difference. [*ETIS* 127]

18. There is no greater indictment of modern principles than the

consequences of those very principles.

The task of the reactionary of today is really an easy one. One only needs to gesture toward the world around us in order to prove how wretched and miserable it is. The most passionate and articulate critique of the modern world can ultimately add very little to that which is plain for anyone to see. We really have little need to argue against technology, industrialism, capitalism, and democracy. Modernity has abundantly demonstrated—nay, proudly celebrated—its own failures. [*ETIS* 155]

19. **Modern man destroys more when he creates than when he destroys.**

The ruins of the modern world pile up all around us. Our destructive capacity grows with every new technological innovation. Industrialism ravages nature; capitalism devastates community and society. The might of modern weaponry could wipe out all life on earth with the push of a button. Wisdom, godliness, health, art, and happiness have been all but eradicated from the world. The greatest tragedy in this fact, however, is not the loss of what is beautiful and good, but the creation of what is wretched and wicked.

If modern man only destroyed what he found, his crimes would be greatly lessened. The true horror is not in the light that he has extinguished, but in the darkness he has cultivated and propagated. That things pass away is part of the natural law; that abominations without number are conjured into being is unnatural and unforgivable. The ruins of something that was beautiful and true retain their dignity and power. The shopping mall built over the rubble is the greater sin. Nuclear waste, "forever chemicals," and microplastics are the product of the creativity of modern man. Destruction is not the unfortunate consequence of mankind's thirst for power, it is the symbol of his victory. [*ETIS* 96]

20. **In an age when the media spews forth a constant stream of inanity, the cultured man is defined not by what he knows but by what he ignores.**

What is there that goes on in the modern world that is worth knowing? To be "informed" in such a world as ours inevitably means to have consumed and digested so much utter stupidity that it has made us incapable of saying or thinking or doing anything that is not stupid. Worst of all, the more news we consume, the more we come to believe that these trivialities are actually important. True ignorance in this age is spectacularly rare and would unquestionably be a blessing. Wickedness and ugliness rarely stem from ignorance, but rather from learning the wrong things. One who thinks he knows something is an infinitely greater threat than one who accepts that he knows nothing. Everyone has an answer, everyone believes they have access to the relevant information. There is an overabundance of opinions and perspectives, but the problem is that none of these subjects are worth having opinions about. We moderns always assume that the more we know about things the better. Is there anything positive in being informed about popular music, the latest television show, social media trends, and the moronic farce we call "politics"? The sage of the modern world simply says: "I don't know anything about that." [*ETIS* 105]

21. **The pessimists foresee a future of collapse, but the optimists are even more horrifying, as they announce the coming of the city of the future, where wickedness and tedium will dwell in perfectly constructed beehives.**

As the scope and scale of the damage the modern world has wrought upon nature becomes increasingly undeniable, we are inundated with hellish visions of doom. Cities will be drowned, farmland will become desert, fires will sweep across the plains, millions will be boiled alive in the heat. Needless to say, climate change is not the only danger that looms. Social strife and disintegration will turn our communities into warzones. The wolf within man will be unleashed. And yet somehow, impossibly, the horrors of this vision are surpassed by that for which we have been told to hope. The march of progress need not be thwarted by collapse, say the optimists, if we can only sufficiently reduce humanity to units of data, which can be arranged in a mechanized system organized by the guiding hand of the technocrat. Faced with a future of barbarousness and savagery or one of soulless automation, it is difficult to say which is more nightmarish. In the end, it may be that we have less to fear from the wolf than from the machine. [*ETIS* 77]

22. **Modern civilization automatically co-opts everything that is in motion.**

Movement is antithetical to tradition. That which travels is, by definition, suitable to the modern mentality. And the faster it travels, the more thoroughly it accommodates progress. That which is grounded, fixed, and immobile presents an inchoate challenge to the modern. Motion is vertiginous and destabilizing. It erodes ties to the land, to nature, to the sacred, and to community. Modern man thinks that he can escape from history and himself if only he can run away from it fast enough and far enough. In this, like so many other gifts of the modern world, he finds too late that he has been caught in a trap. [*ETIS* 168]

23. **While the problems are very grave, they are exacerbated by the number of incompetents democracy summons to solve them.**

It appears to be something of a rule that we moderns are determined to do everything possible to solve a problem other than stop doing the thing which caused the problem in the first place. Modern humanity does more harm in trying to solve problems than it ever possibly could through malice. Certainly an element of this fact can be explained by problems of means and ends, but even more so by the most fundamental characteristic of the modern age: its sense of time. Everything that occurs is an improvement on what has come before. Thus, there could not possibly be an inherent problem created by us moderns. No, all problems can be solved by tinkering. It was not a problem—insists the modern—in its conception but only in its implementation. The modern does nothing if not tinker, that is to say, he is unwilling to accept that he has made a mistake. Hence modernity exists in the worst kind of stasis. When a problem arises, we throw money at it, we throw bureaucrats at it, and we bring the weight of the system to bear against it. Never mind the fact that these things are precisely the root of the problem. [*ETIS* 31]

24. **Modern society is simultaneously becoming increasingly inhospitable to the old while multiplying their number by prolonging their lives.**

A defining character of the modern world, as René Guénon brilliantly pointed out, is the emphasis of quantity over quality. Modern society orients its energies toward the quantitative elements of human life at the expense of the qualitative. Goods can be obtained at low costs by a very high proportion of individuals—but only by reducing the quality of those goods. An enormous number of people in society are given nominal political power—but the nature of that power is so limited that it ultimately comes to nothing.

There are few better illustrations of this principle than modern society's attitude toward the elderly. As the implicit goal of science is the indefinite extension of human life, little to no attention is paid to the quality of human life. Science can enable modern human beings to live longer than previously imagined, but it can do nothing to give their lives meaning or joy. We must ask then: What is the value of longevity in and of itself? [*ETIS* 179]

25. **The prophet who accurately diagnoses the rising corruption in a society discredits himself, because the more corruption grows, the less the corrupt notice it.**

As the Daoist sages put it, the fish is not aware that he is swimming in water until he is gasping for air on land. So, too, is our society increasingly unaware of the murky waters in which it swims. When corruption and degeneracy is universal, one who gestures toward it becomes a pariah. Those who have unquestionably accepted the state of things are more invested than anyone in continuing to insist that all is as it should be. As life becomes unbearable, questioning it becomes unthinkable. We need only look at the example of Christ to see that this is the case. Those who publicly warn against the sins of humanity are reviled and crucified. [*ETIS* 71]

26. **One who renounces only appears powerless to one who lacks the capacity to renounce.**

It is a truism among the leftists and progressives that if one perceives a problem in the world, one is obliged to act to change it. Thus, we see the phenomenon of those who claim to despite what they see in society drowning themselves in it. The fact of the matter is that those who claim to want to change the world are actually entirely invested in maintaining the status quo. What would there be for them to fight against? What glorious struggle would be left for them to engage in, if things really changed? The Promethean instinct is always to fight against things the way they are. Naturally, once all the perceived enemies have been defeated, the firing squad circles around and turns the rifles on itself. One who abdicates or renounces has not lost the struggle; he has recognized it for what it is: a distraction at best, a revolt against the gods at worst. It makes perfect sense that renunciation would be unthinkable to the materialistic modern mentality. We are conditioned to think that victory, like everything else, only has value in material terms. The one who sacrifices gains is a dupe, a fool. As it turns out, it may be that the struggle to renounce is the only struggle that makes any difference in the world, that has any value at all. [*ETIS* 30]

27. **Modern man does not love, but takes refuge in love; does not hope, but takes refuge in hope; does not believe, but takes refuge in dogma.**

We moderns have so utterly beggared ourselves that the desperate search for consolation motivates all our actions. The modern experience is reduced to an endless, futile search for relief from the unbearable world we have created for ourselves. Even the most noble sentiments of love, hope, and faith have become shadows of their true selves. They are no longer experienced in and of themselves, but rather as coping mechanisms. There is a pitiful sense of desperation in the modern consciousness. To paraphrase Carl Jung, there is no limit to the lengths humanity is willing to go in order to avoid facing itself. [*ETIS* 83]

28. **Amidst all of the dismal, suffocating structure of the world, the cloister is the only place where one can feel the sunshine upon one's face and breathe fresh air.**

There is a peculiarly perverse quality in the modern world that makes man most wretched when he is most free, and most at peace when he is most restrained. In a world such as ours, restriction and deprivation can only be a blessing. Does our present degree of freedom enable us to live more joyfully, with more meaning, with more vitality, or with greater reverence for the sacred and divine? In this world, freedom only means freedom to suffer. Thus, the cloister, a space of isolation and renunciation, truly becomes what it was meant to be: an oasis, a sanctuary against the horrors of the world. Nowhere does this become more clear than among the concrete towers and seething masses of the modern city. [*ETIS* 86]

29. **The power of both the Gospels and the *Communist Manifesto* is fading; the world's future belongs to Coca-Cola and pornography.**

Here, at the end of history, after centuries during which grand ideas and narratives battled for the future of the human soul and society, we find that no one has really won and everyone has lost. Neither the forces of the spirit nor the Promethean materialists have conquered. Both the spiritual ennoblement of man and the utopia of liberation have come to nothing. We might say that in some sense the ethos of capitalism has triumphed. But what remains even of that insidious dogma has lost its veneer. Whatever may have once been persuasive in the fantasy that a free market will drive innovation, or result in greater degrees of material prosperity, has now been clearly replaced by the most bland consumerism and abject vulgarity. The collective dreams of humanity have culminated in the fulfillment of only our basest appetites. And thus the world dims to twilight. [*ETIS* 477]

30. **It is never possible to solve a problem well, but it is always possible to solve it worse.**

On what basis do we presume to judge and act? Given what we are, it can come as no surprise to see our projects so often come to nothing. Moreover, it seems that the more vigorously we apply ourselves to an enterprise, the more likely it is to fail. When we realize upon how little our assumptions are founded, we are no longer surprised by failure. A new conclusion is likely to be just as misguided as the one it replaced, if we arrive at it through the same avenues. Montaigne once wrote: "Pride and curiosity are the two scourges of our souls. The latter prompts us to poke our noses into everything, and the former forbids us to leave anything unresolved and undecided." (91) The more we tinker, the more we allow our actions to be guided by our own measure of truth, the further from the path we stray. [*ETIS* 372]

32. The cause of the modern disease is the belief that man can cure himself.

Humanity does not have the power to fundamentally address its own problems. Why should this not be so? If we recognize that we have a problem, then how can we expect ourselves to provide the solution? It would not be much of a problem if someone who suffered from it were able to make it go away just by wanting it to do so. That man, as an individual, is capable of change and healing is clear. But this healing is not achieved at the hands of others who are sick with the same disease. When man looks for answers in his own head, he looks to himself and finds nothing. When man looks in his soul, he finds God and discovers a wisdom and a peace that he could never provide for himself because he does not possess it. As Maistre observes: "The more human reason trusts in itself, the more it seeks to draw all its strength from itself, the more absurd it is, the more it reveals its impotence." (194) [*ETIS* 249]

33. When nothing in society is worthy of our respect, we ought to cultivate, in solitude, new silent loyalties.

We are not bound to accept the realities of modern society as the boundaries of thought. Nihilism, in this age, is more tempting than ever. The great ideas of the past have been struck down and none of the new ones are capable of inspiring us. In the province of the soul, however, we can still swear allegiances, consecrate bonds, and keep faith. Like Spengler's lonely Roman soldier, holding fast at a doomed outpost with no hope for relief, we can and must hold true to our values, even when we are the last ones in the world to do so. So armored, the cultured soul can withstand any force that this wretched world can bring against it. [*ETIS* 352]

34. **Modern man is comforted by the idea that "everything has a solution." As though there were no sinister solutions!**

The most horrific crimes in modern history have always been presented in their time as solutions. Hitler is the prime example of this, along with Stalin and Mao. Modern man refuses to accept that there are no solutions and that even the idea of a "solution" is misguided. The authentic reactionary does not seek to restore what has been lost in the social or political world, thus fixing a perceived problem. The authentic reactionary merely opposes whatever he is presented with. He sees the errors in all proposals and suggests none in their place. The prospect of solving problems does not comfort him. Only the beauty of his dreams can do that. [*ETIS* 350]

35. **God preserve us from all forms of purity—the mother of political terrorism, religious sectarianism, ethical severity, aesthetic sterility, and philosophical inanity.**

In general, the only way to reduce the complex and paradoxical nature of things is to torture them: to flay them alive, to disfigure them, to cut out and throw away anything that does not appear to fit in. What we are left with after this macabre process is a creature that has been made repulsive and hateful by its mistreatment. In the very ugliest things of this modern world, we can perceive the victims of the impulse toward purity, which is in turn enslaved to the human mania for control. To call something "impure" is to identify qualities within it that do not conform to our hopelessly restricted conception of the thing. Paradox, in the final analysis, is but a way of acknowledging the mystery of the world, and the fact that human knowledge is necessarily limited. If one thing bears the properties of another in some mixed proportion, the only error is in our failure to understand how it properly fits into a greater whole and a higher degree of order. [*ETIS* 216]

36. **One should strive to live with clarity: a simple, quiet, discrete life, surrounded by intelligent books, loving but a few precious souls.**

The horrors of the modern world do not infringe upon our ability to live a good and happy life. What has been lost in society or in nature can be reconstructed, on a smaller scale, in our own lives. To find joy and to be in the presence of the divine and sacred is still possible. But in order to do so one must realize that the outside world cannot provide what we desire. The temptation and wickedness of the modern world only exacerbate the dilemma. Certainly, if we covet power, wealth, and the trappings and comforts of technological society, we are doomed. There is no degree of inner strength or will that can preserve us if we allow ourselves to drown in modern culture. If we turn our backs on the fuss and misery that surrounds us, however, we may find yet a modicum of tranquility. The best of mankind is to be found in the wisest books, untouched by the stupidity of modern culture. In these books there is a balm that never loses its potency. To love deeply those who are dear to you, no matter how few in number, nourishes the soul so that it can withstand even the most inhospitable climate out of doors. [*ETIS* 96]

37. **Material prosperity is less degrading than the intellectual and moral requirements for obtaining it.**

In and of itself, wealth need not be a corrupting influence. It tends to be so, of course, but this is primarily due to the actions and the mentality required for accumulating wealth in the first place or for continuing to accumulate it. The problem is, as Burckhardt describes it, the "mania" for money: the fanatical hunger for wealth, which supplants all other desires. Action is no longer motivated by any "inner necessity," in Burckhardt's phrase, and society becomes a battleground of all against all, as each member desperately tries to gobble up his share of the pie before someone else gets to it first. [*ETIS* 202]

38. **The modern tragedy is not the tragedy of reason vanquished, but of reason triumphant.**

As the catastrophic destiny of the modern world becomes clear, man tries desperately to identify where it all went wrong. If only we had followed this path or the other. When something goes wrong, the modern assumes that his calculations were incorrect. He returns to the laboratory, to tinker with his creations, assuming that if only this gear would be put in its proper mechanism, everything would fall into place. "There has been a mistake," he declares. But modern man fails to perceive that all has gone precisely according to his plan. From the beginning, the plan *was* the mistake. It is not that logic and reason have been misapplied. Goya was wrong: it is not the sleep of reason that produces monsters—there is no greater monster than reason itself. Mankind has always battled monsters; reason is the only one against whom there can be no hope for victory. [*ETIS* 113]

39. **In certain ages the spirit loses, no matter who wins.**

The degradation of the modern world is so complete that it is increasingly meaningless to take sides in modern conflicts. Even when one side proclaims itself as the enemy of the things we hate, we can be sure that its victory would bring us no closer to that which we desire. No matter what one says they are fighting for or against, the prize they seek is the same. There can no longer be said to be sides at all because there is an essential unanimity in the modern world. And any dissension from this unanimity would be immediately co-opted by one or another of the parties that desires its preservation. When the instruments of battle are so thoroughly corroded, the battlefield so compromised, and the spoils so tainted, the only meaningful victory would be to refuse to fight at all. [*ETIS* 247]

40. **The loneliness of modern man in the universe is the loneliness of a master surrounded by silent slaves.**

In the early chapters of his *Phenomenology of Spirit*, Hegel introduces one of his most profound concepts: the dialectic of lord and bondsman, or master and slave. The slave produces and the master consumes. Over time the master realizes that for all his power, he is ultimately in the weaker position because the only power he possesses is the power to reduce the other to nothingness. Man desires recognition and yet, to be recognized by one you have debased provides no satisfaction.

Modern man has arrived at a similar position of domination. If man is all powerful and all matter is subservient to him, what hope can he entertain for recognition? Modern man denies all other agency in the cosmos. The world, conceived of as raw material for his appetites, loses all meaning and with it man's power is equally worthless. He is the lord of a barren kingdom, and there is no one left to celebrate his triumphs or crown him with laurels. [*ETIS* 113]

41. **In this century, the individual seeks out the vitality of the crowd to shelter himself from the withering cold that blows forth from the wreckage of the world.**

Solitude is one of the many joys that modern man has lost. The romantics were connoisseurs of solitude. With that far-reaching Spenglerian gaze, the solitary man looked out at the ever-receding horizon, toward infinity. In solitude and stillness, the transient things of this world placidly arrange themselves. Now, however, in solitude man is only overwhelmed with the immensity of his loss. Where once nymphs and elves frolicked on the edge of twilight, there is ruin and desecration. Little surprise then that modern man in this late hour cannot bear to be alone. He is left only with his crimes, and, in his desperation, he hides himself among the multitude. He confuses the riotous and self-righteous spirit of the mob with warmth and comfort. It is all he has. If suffering in a crowd is not diminished, at least it is easier to ignore. [*ETIS* 131]

42. **In both bourgeois and communist countries, "escapism" is condemned as a solitary vice, as a debilitating and vile perversion.**

Modern society discredits the fugitive so no one will pay attention to the tales of his adventures. Art or history, man's imagination or his tragic and noble destiny—these are not criteria tolerated by modern mediocrity.

"Escapism" is a fleeting vision of abolished splendor and an implacable judgement against today's society.

To paraphrase Ursula Leguin: We condemn escapism, but what else should a prisoner do but try to escape? It's not enough that we are imprisoned and suffocated in a soulless, oppressive nightmare of tedium and horror—modern society insists that we do not try to escape or even suggest that there is anything or anywhere to escape to! What is the content of so-called escapism if not a vision of another world, a better world? In this sense, modern society is right to condemn the escapists, for their fantasies are the most powerful possible condemnation and indictment of modern society. [*ETIS* 67]

43. **In spiritually barren ages, the only man to recognize that the world is dying of thirst is one who can still draw from the underground well.**

One who has never experienced joy cannot know that he is miserable. One who has never tasted water cannot know thirst. Modern man, utterly disconnected from his spiritual self, does not realize what he is missing. To be sure, he experiences this absence in countless ways, but he does not understand it. He experiences it as depression, anxiety, neurosis, addiction, and so on. And, needless to say, he drives himself mad unsuccessfully trying to solve those ailments, because ultimately they are but symptoms. Modern man attributes these problems to his unique circumstances and assumes that fundamentally there is nothing *wrong* with society or humanity as a whole. When misery and dejection are universal, joy becomes a meaningless concept. Small wonder, then, that so many millions confuse trivial pleasures and entertainments for genuine happiness. They have never known anything else. [*ETIS* 448]

44. **Man says that truth is relative because he calls his countless mistakes truths.**

Modern man is at least correct in thinking that if there is no objective truth, then any idea—no matter how stupid or harmful—is as valid as any other. Surrounded by false ideas, modern man concludes, sensibly, that there must be no such a thing as one that is unconditionally true. This is how rationality ends by turning in on itself and leads to nihilism. Ideas generated exclusively by means of human reason are ultimately picked apart by that very faculty of reason. If the foundation of a building has nothing to secure it, the structure will invariably collapse. We live in an age now when any possible idea is given an equal claim to validity. Man's thought should be altered according to the truth, but modern man alters the truth to suit his thought. [*ETIS* 334]

45. **The three enemies of humanity are: the devil, the state, and technology.**

Only with the greatest difficulty is man capable of discerning the identity of his true enemies. As a rule, the most dangerous enemy arrives in the guise of a friend. From the devil, who assiduously answers our prayer; to the state, which claims to act on our behalf; to technology, which satisfies our every appetite and desire—those that seek to destroy us always come bearing gifts. Incidentally, this is also how we may identify our true friends: God comes to us empty-handed, offering nothing. [*ETIS* 167]

46. **The most serious charge against the modern world is its architecture.**

The critique of the modern world can be reduced to this one simple point: look at this world, look at how ugly we have made it. How can such a world, so boring and uninspiring, possibly be right or true? All the words of the greatest reactionary thinkers of the past several hundred years cannot equal the impact of staring at a shopping plaza, a hospital, a library, or a suburban neighborhood. Why should our buildings be beautiful? Who cares, it's just a building. Nothing could be so nihilistic as this sentiment and nothing so emblematic of the modern attitude. If this is how we design houses, what does it say about the manner of people we expect to inhabit them? [*ETIS* 294]

47. **To swim against the current is not foolish if the waters are flowing toward a waterfall.**

Quietism does not require us to tacitly affirm the values of a fallen and degraded society, but only to accept that our hostility toward this society should not result in some sort of action to try to change a course that we know cannot be averted. No thinking, feeling soul can do anything but hate this society, and to be fundamentally at odds with it is a prerequisite for any claims to wisdom or decency. We know where this society is headed, we can see its final destination. In fact, we may have already arrived. As the masses pull us closer and closer to destruction, we cannot but seek to go the other way. In doing so, however, we must recognize that our own personal attempts to salvage some modicum of truth will do nothing to alter the destiny of the world. [*ETIS* 331]

48. **Even small-town grudges are more civilized than the mutual indifference of big cities.**

The hostility of the urbanite toward everything rural and parochial goes back at least as far as ancient Rome. The city dweller is educated, sophisticated, and open-minded, while the rustic is ignorant and prejudiced. It is not that these characterizations are inaccurate, but they fail to properly account for the implications and consequences of these modes of life. If the rural man is ignorant, his ignorance is restricted to world events, which he is correct in assuming have no bearing on his life. Where the world he inhabits is concerned, he is profoundly knowledgeable to the level of expertise. If he is prejudiced, his prejudices are generally the product of intimate acquaintance and familiarity. It's easy to not be prejudiced when you have never met someone who is different. In urban areas, people simply ignore those who are different. In a small town, at least people actually know each other, even if they don't get along. [*ETIS* 364]

49. **In the absence of all traces of feudal bonds, the increasing social isolation of the individual and his increasing hopelessness**

ultimately dissolves him into the totalitarian mass.

It is clear that the individual only surrenders his individuality and becomes a member of mass society when there is no longer any meaningful way for him to fit in. The circumstances of the serf, rigid and stratified though they may be, offer integration into a social order, which gives him purpose and community. He understands himself as a part of the whole because his role is clearly defined and, yes, restricted. In the face of countless horrors committed by isolated and hopeless individuals, society desperately tries to figure out ways to make people feel valued, to help them feel that they are a part of something. But what is this something they are supposed to be a part of? The modern world can offer nothing more than abstractions like "humanity" or "society" or "nation." [*ETIS* 429]

50. **Resistance is pointless when the modern world plots to destroy everything that is worthy of admiration. We always retain, however, an incorruptible soul, with which we may contemplate, judge, and disdain.**

That we cannot fight against the forces of the modern world is clear. We have no ground upon which to stage such a confrontation. There is no favorable terrain for the battle against modernity. There are no stratagems that could be more conniving and deceitful than the ones employed by our enemy. There are no weapons more terrible than the ones he yields. To resist is precisely to accept the terms of the victor. Only the one who refuses to meet on the field of battle at all can achieve any meaningful result. There is nothing left to fight for. The souls of communities are, in most places, lost forever. The soul of the individual, however, persists. Upon this hallowed ground, from within the sanctuary of the soul, even if we do not fight, we may at least reject, defy, and hate. To recognize that there is no victory against the modern world is not the same as tolerating or accepting it. [*ETIS* 98]

Works Cited

Benoist, Alain de. *On Being a Pagan.* Translated by Jon Graham; edited by Michael Moynihan. North Augusta, S.C.: Arcana Europa, 2018.

Burckhardt, Jacob. *Judgments on History and Historians.* Translated by Harry Zohn. Boston: Beacon, 1958.

Burke, Edmund. *Letters on a Regicide Peace: Letters I and II.* London: Bell and Sons, 1893.

Burke, Edmund. *Reflections on the Revolution in France.* Edited by L. G. Mitchell. Oxford: Oxford University Press, 2009.

Chesterton, G. K. *Orthodoxy.* Moscow, Id.: Canon, 2020.

Claudel, Paul. *Five Great Odes.* Translated by Jonathan Geltner. Brooklyn: Angelico, 2020.

Dante Alighieri. *The Divine Comedy,* vol. I: *The Inferno.* Translated by Mark Musa. London and New York: Penguin, 2003.

Davis, Michael Warren. *The Reactionary Mind: Why "Conservative" Isn't Enough.* Washington, D.C.: Regnery Gateway, 2021.

Eichendorff, Joseph von. *Ahnung und Gegenwart.* Munich: DTV, 1982.

Eliade, Mircea. *The Sacred and the Profane: The Nature of Religion.* Translated by Willard R. Trask. New York: Harper & Row, 1961.

Ellmann, Richard. *Yeats: The Man and the Masks.* New York: Norton, 1978.

Gandhi, M. K. *Hind Swaraj or Indian Home Rule.* Revised edition. Ahmedabad: Navajivan, 1939.

Galindo Hurtado, Mauricio. "A Reactionary in the Andes: An

Intellectual Biography of Nicolás Gómez Dávila." Master's Thesis, University of Sussex, 1999.

Ghosh, Amitav. *The Great Derangement.* Chicago: University of Chicago Press, 2016.

Gómez Dávila, Nicolás. *Escolios a un Texto Implícito: Selección.* Bogotá: Villegas, 2005.

———. *Notas: Unzeitgemäße Gedanken.* Foreword by Martin Mosebach. Translated by Ulrich Kunzmann. Berlin: Matthes & Seitz, 2005.

———. "El reaccionario auténtico." *Revista Universidad de Antioquia* 240 (April–June, 1995): 16–19.

———. *Scholia to an Implicit Text.* Translated by Robert Pinzón. Bogotá: Villegas, 2013.

Guénon, René. *The Essential Rene Guenon.* Edited by John Herlihy. Bloomington, In.: World Wisdom, 2009.

Hegel, G. W. F. *Phenomenology of Spirit.* Translated by A. V. Miller. Oxford: Oxford University Press, 1977.

Hervier, Julien. *The Details of Time: Conversation with Jünger.* Translated by Joachim Neugroschel. New York: Marsilio, 1995.

Jaspers, Karl. *Man in the Modern Age.* Translated by Eden and Cedar Paul. Garden City, N.Y.: Doubleday, 1957.

———. *Psychologie der Weltanschauungen.* Berlin: Springer, 1919.

Kinzel, Till. "Aphoristic Thought, the Problem of Reading and the 'Implicit Library': Reflections on Nicolás Gómez Dávila." In *Coloquio en el centenario de Don Nicolás Gómez Dávila (1913–2013)*, edited by Diego Pizano. Bogotá: Ediciones Uniandes, 2013. Pp. 22–32.

———. *Nicolás Gómez Dávila: Parteigänger verlorener Sachen.* Fifth revised and expanded edition. Rückersdorf: Lepanto, 2023.

Klages, Ludwig. *Mensch und Erde: Fünf Abhandlungen.* Munich: Müller, 1920.

Llull, Ramon. *The Book of the Order of Chivalry.* Translated by Noel Fallows. Woodbridge: Boydell, 2013.

Maistre, Joseph de. *Major Works, Vol. 1.* Translated by Edward Maxwell III. Perth: Imperium, 2021.

Montaigne, Michel de. *Essays.* Translated by J. M. Cohen. New York: Penguin, 1958.

Montaigne, Michel de. *The Complete Works of Montaigne: Essays—Travel Journal—Letters.* Translated by Donald M. Frame. Stanford: Stanford University Press, 1948.

Moriarty, John. *Dreamtime.* Revised and expanded edition. Dublin: Lilliput, 1999.

Nietzsche, Friedrich. *Beyond Good and Evil.* Translated by R. J. Hollingdale. London and New York: Penguin, 1990.

———. *Twilight of the Idols* and *The Anti-Christ.* Translated by R. J. Hollingdale. London and New York: Penguin, 2003.

O'Brien, Connor Cruise. "Passion and Cunning: An Essay on the Politics of W. B. Yeats." Excerpted in *Yeats's Political Identities: Selected Essays*, edited by Jonathan Allison. Ann Arbor: University of Michigan Press, 1996. Pp. 29–56.

Pope, Alexander. *An Essay on Criticism.* London: Lewis, 1711.

Spengler, Oswald. *The Decline of the West: An Abridged Edition.* Edited by Helmut Werner; translated by Charles Francis Atkinson. Oxford:

Oxford University Press, 1991.

———. *Man and Technics: A Contribution to a Philosophy of Life.* Translated by Charles Francis Atkinson. New York: Knopf, 1932.

Thomas à Kempis. *The Imitation of Christ.* Translated by Aloysius Croft and Harold Bolton. Milwaukee: Bruce, 1940.

Yeats, William Butler. *The Collected Poems of W. B. Yeats.* Edited by Richard J. Finneran. Second revised edition. New York: Scribner, 1996.

———. *On the Boiler.* Dublin: Cuala, 1971.

Printed in Dunstable, United Kingdom

77836306R00147